Presents

Colin Moone's

Published by
THE X PRESS, 55 BROADWAY MARKET, LONDON E8 4PH.
TEL: 0171 729 1199   FAX: 0171 729 1771
E-MAIL: Xpress @ maxis.co.uk

© Colin Moone 1996.

All the characters, company names and events in this book are totally
fictitious and any resemblance to real life persons, or companies with the same
or similar names, is purely coincidental.

All rights reserved. No part of this book may be reproduced in any form
without written permission from the Publisher.

Distributed by Turnaround, 27 Horsell Road, London N5 1XL
Tel: 0171 609 7836

Printed by BPC Paperbacks Ltd, Aylesbury, Bucks.
ISBN 1-874509-18-2

This story is dedicated in loving memory of my mother whose inspiration still burns within me and drives me towards my goals.

PROLOGUE

For the second time since he had first entered the room the man winced nervously under the deep, apparently benign, gaze of his host. There was nothing he could have specifically pointed out in the room which caused the feeling of discomfort in his stomach. The wooden table was like any wooden table, the walls of the small thatched-roof building were bare and built with a mix of the same earth as that which lay under the soles of his workman boots. Even the near darkness, broken only by the flicker of a flame down in the far left corner, couldn't explain why his whole body was shuddering despite himself. He felt cold. Rubbing his sweaty palms together nervously, the man forced himself to look up.

"Is this what you really want?"

That voice again—cool, exuding kindness, almost unconcerned.

He had to, there was no other way. Dry throated, the man breathed in and nodded.

"Yes."

"Then give me what you have in your bag."

Shakily, too hurriedly, the man tipped the contents of the paper bag that was on his lap over the table. Black, bony and pliable in the

1

diffused glow from the candle on the dirt below, the fingers carefully took hold of the item and felt it before putting it down.

Now all the weight of his mission was bearing down on him, he could feel it already. He was as near to physical weakness as a man of his strength had ever felt. It had surely started to show, because the kind voice came out again.

"You feel a'right? Drink some water, man."

Strangely, the man realized his whole attention had been, for a little while, focusing on the half-filled glass of water on the table. He was desperate for a drink from it. The more he could feel a cramp developing inside his stomach, the more he saw the clear cool liquid in front of him as the way to relieve it. Hastily, he reached out and gulped down a mouthful of water, soothing his dry throat like it had never been soothed before. Then he sighed—a long, drawn-out sigh of satisfaction.

"You can go now... I will take care of everyt'ing."

Relieved, the man quickly stood up, nodded, his heavy face tense in the dark. All had been said, he had fulfilled his mission and now he felt an intense desire to leave the smiling scrutiny of that compassionate face, to get away from the building and, yes, to flee the area. For in all the years of his rather trying life he had never felt such a rush of fear as tonight.

In two quick steps, he was at the door. Without a word of farewell, the man stepped out and once outside actually ran the few yards to the dense shrubbery. A succession of rapid glances, left right and behind, then he pushed through the unfamiliar bush, running steadily, until at last he reached the dirt track which snaked down Stylehut Hill. Running as fast as he could, the man covered the few miles of track through to the gully which cut across the lush swath of cultivated lowlands. Now that his business here was complete he felt uncomfortable and nothing but nothing could make him want to stay.

2

ONE
The Sign of Things to Come

Ella groaned as her tiny frame fell to the ground and she hit the thick dirt with a thud. With one eye she peered up at the dazzling hot sun dancing carelessly in the clear blue Jamaican sky. Beneath her she felt the ground rumble as the sound of running feet approached. She tasted the trickle of blood from her lip and clearly heard some sniggering nearby.

"Wha' you do dat for?" her brother's voice cried out.

"Do wha'?" another voice replied innocently.

"Do wha'? Me will give you do wha'... "

Ella listened as her brother's voice trailed away followed by a sudden scuffle which lasted for less than a minute before coming to an abrupt end with the sound of a boy crying.

"Come," Bill said, taking Ella's hand and pulling her up. "You a'right?"

Ella rose to her feet shakily. "Yeah," she replied, putting on a brave face, despite the sharp sting of a grazed knee and the taste of the dirt which covered her hair and uniform. The fall had winded her and her bottom lip was throbbing from the cut.

But she wasn't going to cry if she could help it.

When she looked up she saw the Johnson boy, red-eyed and humbled, stumble away, cussing under his breath that this wasn't the end of the matter.

"Wha' you do to Syd Johnson, Bill?"

Bill shrugged his shoulders. "Nuh much, Sis. Me jus' rough him up a bit—that's all. Me teach him fe pick 'pon someone him own size."

At twelve years old, Ella was small for her age and her baby face made her look even younger. But what she lacked in size she usually made up for in speed. And when her speed couldn't help her, as on this occasion, Bill would be there to pick up the pieces. She gazed proudly at her tall brother and a small smile lit up her face. Bold as she could be sometimes, Bill was always around to protect her if she came unstuck.

Syd and Bill were both fourteen, but Bill towered over the skinny Johnson boy who liked bullying the younger pupils. As Ella now recalled, Syd had tripped her up in the middle of the lunch-break and sent her sprawling in the dirt for no apparent reason. She remembered a similar incident from the week before when he had also confronted her on the school grounds. Then, Syd had given her some cryptic message for her mother which Bill had told her to forget about. He'd said it wasn't important, but now she wished she could remember it. It might have given her a clue as to what was going on. Something was going on, she was certain of it. She just had to find out what.

Ella dusted down her skirt and blouse and limped behind her brother towards the school building, wincing with every step at the sharp sting of the wound on her knee. She stole a quick glance back at the crowd of children who had gathered too late to see the action. In their midst was an unrepentant Syd Johnson, sneering maliciously and making threatening gestures with his hands and arms. Ella was too young to understand the full meaning of Syd's curses, but she caught the general drift.

"What 'appen here?" Mr. Brown's voice boomed in his bilingual mix of formal English and local patois. Standing in the doorway of his classroom, he cut a burly and imposing figure which always commanded respect and sometimes terror among his youthful charges. He looked Ella up and down with a displeased expression. She, still in a dishevelled state, avoided eye contact, embarrassed for once at being in the spotlight of her favourite teacher's glare.

"Cat have yuh tongue?" Mr Brown asked her sternly. "Why you dutty up yuhself so?"

Ella continued staring at the ground uncomfortably.

"Sorry, Mr Brown," Bill interjected, "Ella fall over an' she inna 'nuff pain. Me can tek her home?"

Mr Brown looked up to the heavens and sighed, exasperated. He studied Ella for a moment and accepted that she must be in some discomfort, for Ella was an enthusiastic pupil and few things would keep her away from class. If it was any other pupil, he wouldn't have given them the benefit of the doubt, but as it was Ella, he would make an exception this once. "Okay," he said finally. "Jus' bring her inside first and clean those cuts."

"Okay, Mr Brown, me will do it right away." Bill pushed his sister's weary body along the school's rugged grounds towards the washroom at the side of the classrooms. "Sir, you have a Band Aid fe her cut?" he called back.

"Band Aid?" Mr Brown repeated. "No boy, go cut one aloe plant and I'm sure it will heal bettah."

From a corner of the dusty play area, a heated argument had broken out between opposite teams of pupils in a hotly contested soccer match. Mr Brown's attention now turned to the noisy rabble and he marched with purposeful strides to separate the two sides, on pain of punishment if necessary, leaving Bill to attend to his sister as best he could.

"Why you nevah say not'n to Mr Brown, El?" Bill asked before going off to find the wonder cactus.

Ella drew away. "Well..." she paused and rubbed her watery eyes with a grubby hand. Even to her brother she found it hard to admit she didn't want the other children to think she ran to Mr Brown for every little thing. People were already teasing her about being 'teacher's favourite'. "Not'n Bill, jus' forget it."

Bill got the message. Ella was stubborn at the best of times and there was no use pressuring her when she was this upset. Pulling out his pocket knife, he went off in search of an aloe plant he had noticed many times on their daily journey to and from school.

Buried deep in the countryside, Hayfield School was just large enough to house the sixty or so children who were fortunate enough to secure a place there and who were divided into four classes of mixed ability. The school consisted of six single-storey buildings, erected cheaply using a mixture of concrete, bricks and very basic local materials. Four of these buildings were joined together in a line. These were the classrooms. At each end of this line of classrooms was a building set apart at a right angle. The one closest to the school entrance was the school office, which was generally used for staff meetings. At the far end was the washroom, for use by both boys and girls. At play-times the school became too small and its pupils were allowed to run carefree on the land adjoining the school building.

The fact that the school doubled as the local church on Sundays was a sore point, especially for Mr Brown who objected to having to teach his class from a pulpit. To be fair, the buildings had originally been meant as a church, with a large hall for services and adjoining buildings for lodgings, storage and Sunday School. After the hall burned down one night ten years previously, the Reverend Willard had promptly rebuilt it and continued his evangelising work among the surrounding communities undaunted. Three months later, a second fire consumed the hall and, the Reverend himself, who had taken to sleeping inside his church. After that, the then recently graduated Mr Brown, who had married Reverend Willard's only daughter, decided he might as well use three of the remaining buildings as a school.

The school was extremely popular and quickly grew in size and reputation, with parents sending their children there from homes as far as five and six miles away. Eventually, Mr Brown's school had grown so much it had taken over the entire church grounds and buildings, but in time the aspirations of a group of religiously-minded neighbours convinced Mrs Brown to let them use the premises once again for weekly services. As Mr Brown's classroom was the biggest, it had to accommodate the congregation on the sabbath and increasingly for ceremonies such as weddings, christenings and funerals.

Ella's grazed knee still stung, but had stopped bleeding by the time Bill returned with a healthy looking stalk of aloe which, after preparing it as he had seen done on several occasions, he applied to the wound. Ella let out a sigh of relief for she, like most of the people in the parish, believed in the plant's ability to suck poison out of a cut and to heal it quickly. Many were those locals who regularly misquoted a passage in the Bible as evidence of the cactus' healing powers.

7

"Come mek we go home," Bill said finally, after tying his handkerchief deftly around his sister's knee.

Ella smiled thankfully, for, whether imagined or by magic, the sting in her knee had ebbed. She got up and followed her brother with a new spring in her step. Now all she needed was to go home.

Mr Brown was ringing the school bell to signal the end of the lunch-break and the start of afternoon classes as Bill and Ella reached the school entrance on their way home. The pupils formed four orderly lines, one representing each class, and stood to attention as Mr Brown inspected them as though they were troops on parade. Then they began swarming back into their classes noisily.

"Yuh family don't run t'ings round yah," Syd Johnson's voice squealed as Ella and Bill made their way out. "My faada going get what he wants. Tell yuh mudda and tell yuh faada— if him nuh drunk somewhere!" And with that he was gone, swept away with the other schoolchildren to whatever afternoon classes he had that day.

Ella looked at Bill with a deeply puzzled expression.

"Wha' him mean him faada going get what he wants, Bill?" she asked innocently as her brother guided her homewards.

Bill looked down at his sister, a frown finding his brow. He knows what this is all about, Ella thought to herself, but he's not going to tell me.

"Is not yuh business, El," Bill said abruptly, as he lengthened his stride, "jus' stay outta it."

Ella hurried to keep pace with her brother. So he does know something. Normally, if she wanted to get some information out of Bill she just had to keep pestering him. Today was going

8

to be no exception.

"Is not fair," she whimpered. "Me always get lef' outta t'ings."

Bill merely mumbled indifferently. Ella tried again. She knew that their families didn't get on and as far as she could remember there had always been a feud between the Butlers and the Johnsons, but in recent weeks the animosity between them seemed to have intensified. Never before had she bothered to find out the cause of the feud but now it was affecting her directly. She turned to her brother and protested that by the time she learned what the fight with Syd Johnson was all about, the whole school would already know. And, she insisted, if Bill cared for her as his sister, he would tell her everything she wanted to know before she died of frustration.

But that didn't work either. Bill was as obstinate as Ella was stubborn. The more she claimed her life depended on finding out everything now, the more he insisted his life depended on her not finding out. Finally, Ella could take it no longer and in a sulky mood hobbled quickly up the hilly track away from her brother.

"Don't go too far, El," Bill shouted after her, but he may as well have shouted it to the mountains for all the attention she paid him. She could be so stubborn at times, but in her position he would probably be exactly the same, he reasoned. He didn't think it was fair to keep things from her, but he really didn't want to tell her about the family feud. Couldn't tell her. To explain that their family was at war with the neighbours would only worry her unnecessarily.

They had made the journey to and from school so many times that they could do it with their eyes closed. Not that they would though, for the route was full of the beauty of the Caribbean countryside. There were flowers of every colour and description and the lush green of the bush flanked their route on either side.

Their half-hour journey home was by way of a narrow and crooked road which snaked its way up and down a rocky hill. Despite its potholes, the craggy hillside track was not a dangerous one, as most motorists manoeuvred along its many twists and turns at little more than a crawl, except for the odd taxi driver chatting animatedly to his passengers as he tried to tackle the road at full speed defying the gods and gravity to pull him down to the bottom of the gully below, instead of trying to avoid passing pedestrians.

The noisy roar of a vehicle approaching was warning enough for Ella and Bill to quickly get off the road and stand on the verge beside until the danger had passed.

Ella continued steadily up the hill. Looking behind her she saw her brother bringing up the rear. If she kept up the cold shoulder treatment maybe Bill would eventually relent and tell her what was going on. And with that thought she smiled to herself and slowed her pace a fraction. If she was going to give him a hard time, she would have to allow him to at least catch up.

The journey home took longer than usual. Thirty minutes after leaving Hayfield School, they had only reached the bridge at Roaring River. The river twisted down from the hills and through the valley. But it seemed as though it was at its fiercest when it reached the bridge here which was why the people in the area had named it so.

Ella waited on the bridge looking down at the water as it rushed by in a thunderous gush down to the sea. She loved being here. Sometimes she would stand on the bridge for hours making paper boats which she would drop from one side of the bridge. Then she would hurry to the other side in time to see them carried swiftly away on the river's winding journey to the sea.

At other times she would write a note to an imaginary friend on the other side of the world, making sure she wrote on it her name and address, and pop it into a rum bottle which after sealing she would slip into the water, hoping it would be found by some other young person with whom she might exchange correspondence.

She had read about it in books and if a man stranded on an island could be rescued after sending a message in a bottle, she was hopeful that one of her letters would reach its destination.

And sometimes she would simply sit on the bridge and forget about time as she dreamt of those distant lands across the ocean she had heard so much about and to which, she hoped, she would one day travel.

For the meantime though, she was in her beloved parish in Jamaica and still didn't know why Syd Johnson kept threatening her.

"Hurry up, Bill!" she called back. Her plan to ignore him had backfired. Normally, Bill would have caught up with her by now and they would have made their peace. They were too close to let any foolishness come between them. This time, however, Bill seemed to be ignoring her also. When she had slowed her pace, he had slowed his as well and remained just as far behind her as he had been earlier. Whatever it was Bill refused to tell her, Ella knew, was pretty serious. But that only increased her curiosity and her determination to get to the bottom of this. It infuriated her that her brother sometimes treated her like his 'baby sister'. Only two years separated them in age and the way she saw it, they were practically twins.

"Wha' wrong?" she asked in a tone of genuine concern as her brother caught up.

Bill pushed his hands deep in his trouser pockets and with a hunch of his shoulders, turned to spit into 'thunder's mouth' below the bridge. "Not'n," he said softly. But he couldn't disguise the worried look on his face.

"Wha' you mean, when you silent so?"

"El," Bill began, with a tiresome expression, "we talk about it tomorrow, a'right? Now, me tired."

Of course that didn't satisfy his sister, but Ella could do no more than continue moping.

The two walked on in silence for a while until Ole Miller's imposing two-storey house came into view, looming large on the road ahead. It was a big concrete house with boarded up windows, and had to be approached through a tall, wooden gate. The once white outer walls had long since yellowed and were now peeling, and a badly chipped concrete path led to the steps of a verandah littered with rubble. The plot on which the Miller house stood was overgrown with weeds and tall grass, a testament to years of neglect. Apart from this, it seemed like most houses in Jamaica. But this house had a story to tell.

It was rumoured that Ole Miller had been locked away in the house for over twenty years, coming out only when he needed to stock up on supplies of fruit and vegetables from the bush, and then only at the dead of night.

No-one knew this for sure though, because no-one had had the courage to check or, if they had, no-one had lived to tell the tale. As a youth, Ole Miller's parents had been unable to control him and despite several thrashings he had carried on being a tearaway and was continuously in and out of jail, particularly once he had grown tall and strong and his father, who had aged, was no longer able to punish him.

When his father died, his tormented mother had been left alone to cope with him. Gradually she began to change; those who knew her claimed to the very edge of madness. She turned her back on friends and shunned visitors to the house. Eventually people stopped calling round and the Millers were left to live their lives alone. Now, though, Ole Miller was the only resident here and, although no-one saw him, the children of the area were all familiar with the legend of how he came out at night to 'nyam' unruly pickney.

The two siblings hurried past the house exchanging nervous glances as they always did when passing it. The house was its usual self. Nothing seemed to have stirred within its walls in living memory. Ella glanced back at it momentarily as it disappeared behind her. "Bwoy!" She let out a sigh of relief. "Dat deh house still give me the duppy shakes every time me pass it."

Bill stared ahead. He was also familiar with the stories about the house on the big bend in the road. The Ole Miller story was common knowledge, but he didn't believe the part about him eating small children. That, of course, couldn't really be true.

"You evah see Ole Miller, Bill?"

"Naa."

"You t'ink him really exist?" Ella asked, picking up a stone and seeing how far she could fling it into the bush on the other side of the track.

"Me t'ink so," Bill answered. "But me wouldn't like fe meet him a night, or anytime."

They continued their journey; turning one more bend in the road, Ole Miller's house vanished from view and from their thoughts. Home was only a short distance away now.

There was nothing special about their home. Most houses

13

around the area were similarly single storey and brick built. At the heart of the Butler home was a large sitting room leading off into the two bedrooms and kitchen. As for a bathroom, there was a standpipe at the bottom of the back yard and toilet facilities even further down. Bill and Ella shared a bedroom, a situation they tolerated because they had to. The kitchen was of a fair size and seemed larger without a stove. Their mother was quite happy to carry on cooking on the open fire in the backyard, the way her family had done for generations, and when she wasn't out in the fields tending to harvest, seemed to spend much of her time in the kitchen either washing or cleaning or planning the next day's chores. Somehow she managed this at the same time as farming the twenty acres of land they owned adjacent to their house, with the help of just one elderly farmhand.

As Ella and Bill approached the fence around their house, Mom Butler came out. By the time they'd reached the gap where the gate used to be, their mother was filling the space.

"Whe' you t'ink you going ah dis time, child?" she demanded of her daughter. She was a mountain of a woman, with a plump face permanently wrapped in a headscarf that dangled down her back. "You hear me, child? Wha' you ah do home so early?" she repeated, turning to Bill.

Ella trembled, her mouth gaped wide open. Her mother's anger always managed to strike her dumb. No thoughts of Ole Miller now—Mom Butler was the danger. Both her children knew what pain their mother could inflict on them with a backhand strike or less. They had felt it many times before and, consequently, always tried their best to avoid her wrath.

"Mom," Bill started nervously, moving out from behind

14

Ella, "Mr Brown send me home with Ella. She fall over an' cut her leg an' her mouth."

Their mother put her hands on her hips. "Wha' you talking about, child?" she demanded, narrowing her eyes threateningly.

Bill gulped hard. The danger was far from over. He was expecting to receive a stinging slap to his ear any moment now. "Ah true, Mom. Mr Brown send me home," Ella confirmed, now that she'd had a chance to pull herself together. "You want me fe bring a note from teacher tomorrow?"

"Nuh bother with dat, me should can trust you by now," Mom Butler replied. "Now you here, there's plenty work fe do before dem deh people from the church come, cause every siddung smaddy got dem 'tan up day."

Bill and Ella looked at each other briefly. Their mother was often talking in proverbs which they didn't always understand. They followed Mom Butler into the house. If people were coming round then Bill would have to go and cut some fresh coconut. He darted into the house to collect his machete and soon reappeared at the back door brandishing the weapon, sneaking a quick wink at Ella as he whisked past her.

"Me can go with Bill, Mom?" Ella asked sheepishly. With her mother in such a foul mood she only half-expected to be allowed out, but she didn't feel like staying home to suffer her mother's anger alone.

"Gwan!" Mom Butler shouted, waving her daughter away.

Ella needed no more encouragement to set off after Bill at a speed which made her mother wonder if she shouldn't ask her to bring a note from her teacher the next day after all.

"Mek sure unuh come back soon," her voice boomed after them. "You haffe help tidy up the place before dem deh people come."

15

Trying to catch up with her brother on his way to Flatgrass, Ella acknowledged her mother with a wave of her hand. Mom Butler had been in a bad mood since the last time their father had been home. That was two days ago. His depressive behaviour, excessive drinking and frequent disappearing acts gave their mother plenty to be upset about. Ella was close to her father and missed him when he was away, but he'd never gotten over the death of his youngest child, Little Jakie, and couldn't bear to be in the house for too long. If only Mom Butler would understand.

Flatgrass consisted of several acres of fertile land used for growing anything and everything. It was owned by the Butlers and carefully looked after by a man nicknamed PickneyDaddy. He was said to have fathered at least twenty children from as many mothers and had grudgingly accepted the name many years before.

PickneyDaddy's parents had originally lived near Flatgrass and had been very close to Mom Butler's parents. However, when PickneyDaddy had still been a boy his parents were killed in a fire. PickneyDaddy had lost not only his parents but his home and any means of support. Mom Butler's family had taken him in and offered him a job working the land. He'd worked there for more than fifty years now, and had his own little shack nearby, a regular evening meal and a few dollars a week pay. PickneyDaddy was happy with the arrangement, because he needed friends more than he needed money. For, even though he was supposed to have all these children, no-one ever visited him. At sixty-five he would have been very much alone were he not an honorary member of the Butler family.

When Ella reached the Flatgrass coconut trees she could see no sign of her brother.

"See me yah!" Bill's voice came suddenly from overhead.

Ella jumped back in surprise. Masking her eyes from the sun, she looked up to see her brother's blurred outline halfway up a coconut tree.

"Hurry up nuh!" she shouted, annoyed at being startled. But Bill was enjoying his prank and instead of making haste, started singing at a leisurely pace:

"It was under the coconut tree, dahling,
It was under the coconut tree,
You promised to marry to me…"

Ella waved him away dismissively. Bill looked down at his sister with a cheeky grin before moving further up the tree.

"You bettah stand back, El!" he called.

"Me safe yah so," Ella replied, standing firm.

"A'right, jus' don't blame me if one ah dem jelly bounce off fe yuh head!"

Bill stretched across the tree and, with his machete, cut down a coconut from the branch. It fell away almost immediately. "Look out below!" he shouted as the young coconut somersaulted in the air before crashing to the ground a few feet from his sister.

"That was close," she screamed. "You do that 'pon purpose."

Bill chuckled to himself as Ella gathered the fallen jelly. He cut a further five jellies, before swiftly climbing down.

"You can manage?" he asked, as Ella juggled with a jelly

under each arm.

"Jus' true you is a bwoy you feel seh me weaker than you?" she replied, kissing her teeth in mock disgust.

Now that he seemed in a better mood she was going to pursue her earlier line of questioning. Maybe this time he'd tell her what she wanted to know.

"You ready fe tell me 'bout Syd Johnson?" she asked, almost pleadingly.

Bill thought about it for a moment before answering. "Naa." Ella kissed her teeth again, this time sulkily. Bill ignored her once again and, instead, rolled the four large jellies together and studied them with the eye of an expert. He then looked up at the ones Ella clasped in her hands, smiled, and stood up. "Me ah bring four back," he announced as he took the two jellies from his sister.

"So wha'ppen to the rest?"

Bill threw the two young coconuts to the ground and began hacking away at one until an opening appeared. He peeled the top away revealing soft, white flesh.

"Me ah go drink dis one," he declared, pushing the coconut up to his mouth and taking a swig from it. The milk dribbled down his chin, wetting his shirt, but Bill didn't seem to notice. When he'd finished, he bent down, picked up the hacked off top of the coconut and, using it like a spoon, began to scoop the flesh out of the drained shell. Only after completely devouring content of the coconut in his hand did he chop open the other one and hand it to Ella.

"Bwoy, me did feel seh you forget me," she said hungrily, before guzzling down the cool drink.

Times like this made Ella realize how lucky she was to be living in the most beautiful place in Jamaica, if not the world. In her view there was nothing more refreshing on a hot, sunny day than a drink of fresh coconut milk. She had often daydreamed in Mr Brown's geography class of far-off places like Paris and Rome and Addis Ababa—romantic places which she one day hoped to visit. But where else could she roam so freely and cut down a coconut when she pleased to quench her thirst? Where else could she have so much fun by simply sitting under a coconut tree with her brother Bill? She tilted her head back and drank one final mouthful of the coconut milk.

"Wha' unuh ah do?" a gruff voice barked suddenly from behind them, shattering the stillness of the moment.

Ella was so startled by the intrusion that she spun her head too fast and nearly choked, and ended up spraying the intruder full in the face with coconut milk.

"Dyam an' blast to hell!" PickneyDaddy shrieked, as Bill thumped Ella on the back to clear the choking, "you haffe spit in me face?"

The old man wiped his face with the sleeve of his shirt. Ella and Bill could not hide the smirks on their faces at the sight of their friend with coconut juice dripping down his chin. PickneyDaddy, however, was not amused.

"You see when someone can't hear," he warned, "dem will feel." And with that he disappeared off in the direction of his home, cursing and flinging his arms into the air like a person not of sound mind.

"Why you upset him?" Bill asked, gathering his machete from the ground.

"Me nevah do it fe spite," Ella protested, wiping her mouth dry.

"PickneyDaddy him a'right. Him always joking 'bout most t'ings, but ah true him vex now."

Ella shrugged her shoulders in resignation and picked up the two remaining coconuts. "Me seh me nevah know ah him

19

deh. Me did 'fraid it was a duppy..."

Bill, with a coconut nestled snugly under each arm, was already strutting homewards. He teased his sister for thinking that a ghost would try to trouble them in the middle of the day. Didn't she know that evil spirits only came out at night?

"Wait fe me nuh." Ella called out. Evil spirit or not, she wasn't too happy about being left out in the middle of the bush after her recent fright.

Mom Butler's beautiful voice floated out as the siblings neared home. When she was alone in the house, their mother would often wash her troubles away with an uplifting verse or two of one of her favourite hymns. "Nearer my God to thee..." she sang as if she had not a trouble in the world now that she had climbed to that fabled mountain top and seen the other side.

The children marched through the half-open front door to find their mother dusting the living room.

"We back, Mom," Bill shouted, resting the coconuts on the ground.

Mom Butler's singing came to an abrupt stop and for a moment her children were able to see the look of embarrassment on her face as if they had caught her doing something she wasn't supposed to. "Is about time unuh arrive. Send out pickney yuh foot rest, but yuh heart nuh rest," she said. "Pick up the jelly an' bring dem come."

Mom's voice was no sooner heard than obeyed.

Bill scooped up his possessions once more and followed his mother into the kitchen where he gently placed them on the table. Ella followed and did the same, then stood for a moment staring out of the window over the table into the backyard.

Their yard was big and near the back door was a small fire surrounded by bricks. On top, staked through, was a half-roasted chicken. On the ground, next to the fire, were three smouldering breadfruits. Elsewhere in Jamaica the twentieth century had brought with it the latest technological advancements, but here in the countryside cooking was mostly done the way it had been a hundred years before.

While her mother was preoccupied with preparation for her guests Ella took the opportunity to sneak out of the kitchen and crept wearily into her bedroom. It was a small room, with a window overlooking the front of the house. She slumped onto her bed and yawned loudly. It had been a long day and she hadn't realized how tired she was until now. She had barely laid her head down before her mother noticed her absence.

"Wha' you ah do sleeping ah dis time child?" Mom Butler bellowed from the doorway suddenly. "Jus' because teacher tell you fe go home, it don't mean you fe come home an' sleep, y'know."

Ella turned over onto her back and stared back at her mother. Their relationship was unusual at the best of times and of late had become especially strained.

Even though Ella knew her mother loved her dearly, she was too young to understand why Mom Butler was uncomfortable and always so harsh with her.

She guessed it had something to do with the death of her younger brother, because before Little Jakie died her mother had been strict but loving. Since the boy's death, Mom Butler had become even more strict and seemed to have no patience for her surviving children. Ella often hoped, and sometimes prayed, that one day the old, loving, Mom Butler would return, but until that day she would remain closer to her father.

"Awww, come on nuh Mom!" Ella retorted.

"Come on whe'?" Mom Butler said. "Me an' you nah go nowhere but the kitchen."

At about five o'clock, when the sun began to slip out of view on the horizon, there was a loud knock at the front door. Mom Butler took one last look around before going to the door and opening it to the three women.

"Oh, Sister Ivy!" Her eyes lit up for the first time that day. "Sister Charmaine an' Sister Nichols," she continued, fussing over the three women and ushering them into the house. "How nice to welcome unuh to my humble home."

Ella, leaning against her open bedroom door, watched the three women as they entered. Sister Ivy, a heavyweight in every sense, was their leader and carried two Bibles to prove it. Her companions were twins, both spinsters, and both devoted to the Lord. Though Sister Charmaine and Sister Nichols together didn't add up to Sister Ivy in size, they were no lightweights either and had been known to use their hardback King James editions as offensive weapons in the impromptu disciplining of more than one disobedient pickney. This evening though, they were on a social visit and weren't expecting to use the good Book for anything other than to praise the Lord.

Mom Butler plucked off their coats and guided the three women into the front room, sitting them down on the settee.

"How nice an' tidy you manage to keep your place," pronounced Sister Ivy, straining her neck to take in as much as possible of the Butler home without shifting her seat.

Mom Butler smiled from ear to ear. Sister Charmaine and Sister Nichols nodded their approval also. One of them said something about cleanliness being next to godliness and that

Satan loved nothing better than to lurk in dirty and untidy homes.

"My, what a way yuh daughter turn big gal!" Sister Ivy beamed as Ella entered the room.

Ella looked around shyly. She hadn't been referred to as a 'big gal' before and decided she quite liked it.

"Hello," she squeaked.

"Bwoy," Sister Nichols agreed, "what a lovely way you grow."

Ella acknowledged the flattery with a smile and turned to Sister Charmaine, expecting her to lavish praise also. Sister Charmaine, who was wedged tightly in the corner of the settee, simply folded her arms and smiled sickly before reminding Ella that it was always best to be humble. "Self-praise is no recommendation," she said.

"Well then," Mom Butler interjected, "gwan nuh Ella, and we'll call you when we ready."

Ella nodded and turned to go in the kitchen.

"Yes, you have a lovely daughter, Mom," Sister Nichols repeated. "You must tek her up to the church more often an' get her into the faith."

"Yes," Mom Butler agreed.

"Yuh see, young people these days nuh waan fe go church an' cleanse dem soul," a serious Sister Ivy said. "Dem jus' interested in running up an' down an' getting into bad company. Nah true, Sister Charmaine?"

Sister Charmaine remained silent but nodded her agreement.

"Is really lovely when we get young ones joining in with us big people, 'cause we can begin fe influence dem behaviour from ah early age," said Sister Nichols. "Otherwise Satan will find work fe idle pickney hands."

23

"Hallelujah!" chirped Sister Ivy. But Sister Nichols wasn't finished yet.

"Too much pickney nowadays believing in duppy more than Jesus. An' not jus' pickney, but dem faada and mudda too. Dem nuh have no fait' so dem leggo prayer an' turning to obeah in sickness an' health. You can't praise the Lawd Sunday morning an' when evening come start talk 'bout how you 'fraid fe duppy. An' you can't aarks the Lawd to guide an' protect yuh family an' then you run gone ah obeah man the moment yuh pickney tek sick."

There was a brief silence. Sister Nichols had touched a delicate point with all of them.

Many were the parish residents who balanced their faith precariously between conventional Christianity and the dark sciences known as obeah; as Pastor Stephenson had regularly pointed out from the pulpit, they were "trying to serve the Lawd an' the Prince of Darkness...you can't serve two masters."

Such were the ways of these simple country people who could be as devout as any Christian out there but had come to depend on more than faith for their harvest. And though people would never admit it openly, many more were those in this parish who turned to the spirit world for day-to-day assistance, than were those who were prepared to simply wait until judgment day.

After a silent pause, Mom Butler said, "me jus' popping to the kitchen, me won't be long." She scurried out of the room with a look of complete relief on her face.

In the kitchen, Ella observed her mother for a moment or two—they were both thinking the same thing.

"Why you invite dem, Mom?"

Mom Butler looked back, as she washed her hands.

24

"Is wha' you want nuh?" Mom Butler asked

"Not'n," Ella said. "I is jus'… me know you nuh like dem, so why you let dem visit?" she asked nervously, unwilling to suffer the consequences of any backchat.

"First, me nevah invite dem, dem invite demself. An' nex', pickney dem mustn't aarks so much question. Me nuh like when unuh pickney talk to me an' gwan so," her mother snapped. "Sweet mout' fly follow coffin go ah hole!"

"People can't jus' invite demself so," Ella insisted, trying to sound helpful. She didn't mind the church women visiting, but when her mother so clearly felt uncomfortable about having to put herself out for three women she hardly knew, Ella couldn't understand it.

"Well," Mom Butler began, rather more subdued than normal, "when me lef' church last week, dem seh dem ah go come down fe get fe know me bettah. You see," she paused for an instant, "the church determined inna its cause, an' often send the worker dem fe spread the word, an' fe mek sure that you firmly committed."

"Yeah, me know, Mom," Ella began, "but dat ah jus' like forcing you fe do somet'ing you nuh waan fe do."

Mom eyed her intensely as if she was studying her for the first time in years. Her daughter was right, a little facety perhaps, but she was right. Ella was growing up fast and was learning the ways of the world quickly as well. Ella too could sense something. This felt like the first normal conversation she and her mother had had in a long while. She thought back to when Mom Butler used to be like this, warm and approachable. But since Little Jakie's death both her mother and Dada had become different people.

"Sister Butler!" came a cry from the other room. "You forget 'bout we?"

"No," Mom Butler called back, drying her hands. "Me soon come."

Ella's and her mother's eyes met briefly, as they exchanged knowing smiles, before Mom Butler disappeared back into the front room carrying a tray with three glasses of cool coconut juice, one for each of her guests.

Through the kitchen window Bill was visible, working hurriedly on the fire in the backyard.

Ella rapped on the window, and he looked up. "You finish yet?"

"Yeah, come yah an' give me a hand," Bill's muffled voice came back. Ella ran outside to find her brother blowing furiously to put out a flame that had caught the corn he was roasting.

"See it deh!" he said proudly, pawing at the burnt bits on the edge of the cob. "Safe."

"Come nuh," Ella said finally, bending down and gathering three well-done pieces of corn. "Pick up the breadfruit before Mom come out looking fe you."

Bill wrapped the large and steaming breadfruits in a napkin before following his sister into the kitchen where he carved up the breadfruits while Ella scraped the burnt edges off the corn with a knife.

With the plates stacked high with a delicious-looking meal of chicken, corn and breadfruit, Mom Butler came into the kitchen to take the tray with the food to the dining room.

"Oh, no!" the children heard Sister Ivy exclaim. "You shouldn't have. We nah stop long."

"Dat ah no problem," Mom Butler replied. "Is only a small snack."

Wiping the untidy work surface, Bill chuckled to himself. "Dem love nyam food but pretend like dem nuh want it."

"Me know," Ella replied, "but dem all like dat."

"Dem?" Mom Butler queried, coming back. "Who is dem?"

"Me seh dat all church people put on dis type ah pure act. Why dem pretend like dem nuh waan eat we food?"

"Child!" Mom Butler hissed. "Wha' sort ah rubbish you ah chat? Giving your soul to Jehovah is not a act. An' jus' fe being so dyam outta order, you ah go church 'pon Sunday!"

With that she was out of the kitchen, bearing more refreshments for her guests.

Ella was humbled by the sudden rebuke and she was still mulling over how she'd get out of going to Sunday Service when there was a thunderous banging at the front door. In the living room Sister Charmaine almost jumped out of her skin, and the glass of coconut water that balanced precariously on her lap slipped to the floor.

"Oh, sweet Jeezus!" This drew sharp looks from Sister Ivy and Sister Nichols. It was only the second time she had spoken, and the response she attracted from her colleagues suggested she shouldn't have opened her mouth at all.

The banging came again, rattling the front door on its hinges. Mom Butler looked anxious and hurried into the kitchen. "Quick Bill, go round the back an' stop him from making dat noise. The dyam fool mussi lost him senses again."

She knew who was at the front door and she was determined that he wasn't going to spoil her afternoon. That was why she had bolted it from the inside the moment her guests had arrived.

Bill darted out of the back door and around the side of the house with Ella hot on his heels.

"Wait nuh," she called.

By the time Ella caught him up he was standing opposite the man who had been banging the front door.

"Wha' you ah do, Dada?" Bill asked.

Their father looked back at his son with eyes that were glazed and unfocused. He was a tall man, on the slim side of well-built, and sported a neat beard on his chin.

Though years of hard toil had endowed him with well-developed leg and arm muscles, a slight paunch suggested Jim enjoyed as much play in life as he did work. He leant forward and exhaled a stream of stale breath that was probably ninety per cent neat white rum. He mumbled something about "a man haffe run t'ings inna him yard", before staggering backwards and then steadying himself to pound the door some more. Bill caught his father's fist in mid-air.

"You stink ah drink!" he observed, too disgusted to fear the consequences. He held his father's wrist tight and rigid and expected to feel Jim's fury at any moment. His relationship with his dad had soured considerably over the last year. As his father's drinking increased, Bill's tolerance of the situation had decreased. There wasn't much the son could do about things, and he hated having to stand by and watch his mum brawling with his dad in his worst moments of inebriation.

When he wasn't drunk, Jim Butler was a very quiet man, hard working and private.

He'd originally come from Seaport and had moved the few miles up to Roaring River when he married a very beautiful Grace Jackson, fifteen years ago. When her parents died soon after, the couple inherited their house and land. But the responsibility of administrating and farming the land was great and soon the marriage began to show the strain.

At the height of their problems, tragedy had struck when a terrible accident robbed them of their youngest son, Little Jakie.

28

It happened only a few months after Jim finally got promoted to driver for the Cane and Tobacco Farm Company.

One morning he took five-year-old Jakie with him to drop him off at his sister's house for the day at her request. Jim made one stop at the rum shop. Though he wasn't that much of a drinker then, he enjoyed the traditional Jamaican nectar like anyone else. How Little Jakie, alone in the cab of the truck for only a couple of minutes, could have managed to slip the handbrake off and caused the truck to roll down into the cliff side, no-one ever satisfactorily explained. Some said Jim Butler forgot to ensure the brake was on; some even alleged that dark forces had been at play in the fatal accident.

The loss of his youngest son, of his new job and of his wife's love all at the same time, turned Jim Butler into a broken man. From that moment Mrs Butler's attitude to everything changed and she became cold and moody. Jim, meanwhile, had buried himself at the bottom of a rum bottle in a vain attempt to obliterate the tragedy from his mind. Over a year had passed since and things were still the same.

"Dada!" Ella cried, running up to him and throwing her arms around his waist.

"You always glad fe see me, El, but yuh brother…"

"Forget dat, Dada," Bill said coldly. "It's jus' dat Mom have people inside."

"Oh, sorry," Jim said sharply, "me nuh good enough fe yuh mudda friend?"

Bill sighed deeply.

"No Dada, not'n nuh go so. You know me nevah mean it dat way. Is jus' church people, an' you have too much fe drink."

Jim glared back at him. "Me nuh need to shame fe wha' me do—at all, at all."

He resented the look of disgust in his son's eyes. He had only had a few drinks and yet Bill was treating him like a leper, in his own home. Where had all the respect gone?

Bill laid the blame for his brother's death squarely at his father's feet. He didn't need to say anything, Jim could see it in his eyes, hear it in the tone of his voice and feel it in his presence. And since Little Jakie's death, Bill had assumed the mantle of the man of the house at every opportunity, only too eager to relieve his father of those duties. Or so it seemed to Jim, who wasn't having any of it and regularly reminded his son that only one king could rule the castle. This time though, Jim considered, a box in Bill's ear would help to ram home the message that he was still a pickney and would remain so for at least another few years.

Ella saw the fury in her father's eyes and was only too aware of how violent a temper he could have when he'd been drinking. She wasn't going to give him the chance to hit her brother, however.

"Listen, Dada," she said quickly, "come mek we go down ah the Swinging Tree 'til dem leave."

Jim continued to glare at his son while Bill did his best to avoid his father's gaze. "You bettah watch wha' you chat, pickney, else a fight going bruk between me an' you," Jim warned him, before taking Ella by the hand and leading her away.

TWO
Fight for Land

The Swinging Tree was Ella's favourite place. It was a massive coconut tree which seemed to her to stretch upwards for miles. Beside it stood another almost identical tree. Through some freak of nature, the bark of both had stripped away from the top and now hung down all the way to the ground. Some years ago, Jim Butler had fashioned the ends of the bark into a seat by cleverly weaving it with some large leaves from a banana tree. The result was a free-swinging seat for his children which was strong and comfortable.

Jim leant uncomfortably against the Swinging Tree, watching his daughter rocking to and fro. They had been engaged in pleasant conversation, just passing the time. He had asked Ella how her day at school had been. She had told him about the fight with Syd Johnson and how she was forced to go home early. Watching her father closely for his reaction, she had added that Bill wouldn't tell her what was going on between their family and the Johnsons. Her father had simply grunted and said something about Syd being a 'devil pickney'.

Then Ella asked her father where he had been these last two days and why he hadn't come home. Jim shifted uneasily, before replying that he had been 'visiting' some people.

"You shouldn't do it Dada," Ella muttered quietly as she swung in front of and then behind him. She hated seeing her father like this. She didn't mind him enjoying a drink or two, but nowadays he was more often drunk than sober.

He frowned at her, his eyebrows sinking deeply into his forehead. "Do wha'?" he slurred, attempting to stand upright without the aid of the tree.

"You know," Ella continued, "drink." She dragged her feet along the ground, and halted the pendulum motion of the swing. "You always drinking too much an' you know how it upsets Mom."

Jim Butler looked perplexed. His mood had suddenly changed, and he wiped a forehead heavy with sweat, even though the sun had long since cooled. He stumbled and stuttered as he tried to conjure up a reply, then turned to confront his daughter.

"Me dear child," he began, "if me tek a few drinks now an' again, dat ah my business!" His words were still slurred, but his anger was clear enough. "Me slave long hard hours fe feed my pickney so when me feel fe enjoy meself, me will. Y'understan'? Some man like fe lick sensi inna dem head, me waan drink me rum—ah so it go." Waving his arms wildly to emphasize the point, he lost his balance and stumbled, only just managing to remain standing. He sighed.

Ella could smell the rum on his breath and saw his eyes were unfocused. "It looking like you have enough already," she said.

Jim smiled as he searched his pockets for his quarter bottle of rum. He found it quickly, glanced at Ella, smiled before tipping the contents down his throat. "Bwoy, what a t'ing strong," he let out a satisfied sigh, gazing at the empty bottle.

Father and daughter had an understanding and no matter how much Jim wanted to be sharp with Ella, his tone soon softened. He wanted to explain things to her and tell her about all the hurt inside of him. He felt sure she would understand. But how could he? It was just too painful.

"Me trying to change, but your mudda don't want to understand...you know, yuh mudda can't forgive me over Little Jakie. Me try hard fe talk to her about it, but she don't waan know."

"Me know, Dada," Ella acknowledged, "she coming like Bill; none ah dem will even mention him name."

"Cho', it nuh matter, El, dem will deal with it in dem own time," Jim slurred. "Do me a favour, run go get PickneyDaddy, so we can have a drink. Ah long time him nuh drink with me... I can't resist the rum bottle. Sometimes I wonder if is not obeah deh 'pon me."

He was rambling now, but Ella's interest was, nevertheless, aroused.

"Is wha' you say 'bout obeah, Dada?" she asked, jumping off the swing and walking towards her father. She didn't know much about it but her mother had always told her that obeah was evil and the very sound of the word made her go cold inside.

Jim Butler suddenly went quiet and seemed to sober. He looked across at Ella for a couple of seconds as if searching for some feasible explanation, and then decided against it. "Nuh worry yuhself," he said wearily before falling down on the grass at the foot of the Swinging Tree.

Ella felt hot blood rush to her head. Once again she was being kept in the dark. Something was going on and the two people in her small world that she felt closest to were keeping the facts from her. She was about to press her father further when a familiar cry echoed through the bush, shattering her opportunity.

"Ella, Mom want you!"

It was Bill's voice calling, but it was too dark to see him at this distance. Father and daughter must have been out there for some time. As always when she was getting close to her father, time seemed to fly past. If Mom Butler was calling for her now, her guests must have gone. She looked down at her father who looked as though he was ready to fall asleep and held out her hand to help him up.

"Come, mek we go home," she suggested.

Jim looked up at his daughter lovingly and smiled. She really did care about him, he thought, as he lifted himself to his feet. He put his arm around her shoulders for support and said quietly, "Nuh worry, me will make sure you is a'right. Not'n bad going happen to my pickney. Trust me."

The quizzical look on Ella's face suggested that his daughter needed more to go on than simply 'trust'. She had to know exactly what was going on and what her father meant by his last statement.

"So you decide fe come home then?" Mom Butler asked accusingly as Jim approached the front door, supported by Ella. He looked at his wife with a sweet smile that quickly disappeared when he saw her frown. She couldn't see what there was to be sweet about. "You finish work t'ree hour ago an' spend all fe yuh time drinking yuh life down ah gully. An' me nah even mention the two day dem me nuh see you."

Ella cringed and sloped away into the house. The

battleground had been prepared and she didn't want to be around when the fighting began. Jim Butler shrugged his shoulders and stared deeply into Mom Butler's eyes. Then he rolled his eyes up to the evening sky above, kissed his teeth, and brushed past her into the house. "Me only go fe a few drinks," he grumbled as he stumbled in.

"A few drinks an' it tek up over two day! How come rum mek woman siddung an' ah consider, but mek man walk an' ah stagger?"

His wife was persistent, he'd give her that. Jim staggered into the kitchen and turned on the tap, filling a chipped mug with cold water. As he watched the running water his thoughts drifted and for a few seconds he wasn't in his kitchen, but in some far away land. His dreamland, where he and his family lived happily ever after. A land where they had no troubles and where he and Mom Butler never argued, but showered all their love on each other and on the children. It was an impossible land where, far from being dead, Little Jakie was alive and well and living life to the full with them.

His imagination hadn't wandered too far when a loud knock at the door brought him back to the here and now and he realized that the mug had overflowed. He turned the tap off.

The front door rattled again.

Mom Butler approached the door and through the shutters could clearly see three burly figures standing outside. She pulled the door open. On the doorstep were the three Johnson brothers: Robert, Syd's dad; Jim Butler's tenant, Kai; and Ivan Johnson. Three dark-skinned big-belly men with unkempt hair and beards and with an air of the bush about them.

"Wha' you waan?" she asked gruffly.

"Yuh husban', if him deh yah Mistress Butler," came a reply from one of the men.

35

Mom Butler called over her shoulder to her husband. Jim came lazily to the door.

"Cho', so you ah come back so? Wha' you waan now?" he growled when he saw them. Ella who had gone straight to her bedroom when she came in, had heard the knocking and was now watching the proceedings from the kitchen door. If she kept quiet and nobody noticed her, she would soon discover what the big secret was.

"We have some business fe finish up Butler," Robert Johnson said gingerly, sucking his lip in. Mom Butler drew back, standing slightly behind her husband. Jim blocked the doorway. These men were uninvited and unwelcome.

"Business? Wha' business?" Jim hissed, casually leaning up against the door frame. "Johnson, you should well know me an' how me feel 'bout you. We nuh have no business fe discuss."

"Me can smell dat you full ah drink, Butler," Robert snorted. "It bettah we come back later."

"You ah go talk business?" Jim Butler's nostrils widened and his face began to glow.

"Wha' exactly you waan talk 'bout?" Mom Butler asked, in an attempt to diffuse a situation that she could see was about to explode.

"Dis ah man business, Mom," Kai muttered, finding something funny to laugh about.

Mom Butler glared at him, unamused.

"No offence, Mom," he said apologetically, raising his hands in submission. "We come fe talk 'bout buying our land."

"You mean seh you Johncrow ah man? Tek a look at yuhself, you nuh fit fe walk 'pon my land, much less buy it!" Mom Butler chided and Kai shrank in humbleness behind his brothers.

"Me tell you a'ready, Johnson, me nah sell a dyam to you," Jim said calmly.

"Why you ah chat so, Butler? Hear nuh," Robert began, then paused for a few seconds. He stepped closer. "The piece ah land me have small. Too small fe mek a living farming. All me want ah some security fe me pickney dem."

"It wouldn't be bad, Johnson, if dat was all you did want. Is not all you want. Lickle by lickle, you want fe tek more ah me land. Dat mean dat Mom's mudda an' faada grave woulda deh inna your piece ah land an' we would haffe aarks yuh permission fe go an' see it. You evah hear somet'ing so stupid? Ah so you love to pop joke, man." Jim pointed an accusing finger at Robert Johnson and laughed, and soon Mom Butler was laughing too.

"Is not a joke Butler," Robert said stroking his beard. "Me need security bad, an' me need fe expand me farm. Me jus' can't deal with t'ings inna dat deh small place." He wiped his brow. "Listen," he began again, "we know the history ah wha' did gwan years ago an'…"

"Johnson," Jim interjected. "You ah talk bad. Me nuh know wha' you ah go seh, but whatever it is, dem deh t'ing deh talk 'bout years ago." Jim had become even frostier. He swung the door agitatedly as if to slam it in Johnson's face.

"Bwoy, you nuh fair," Robert said in resignation. "You, more than anyone else, shoulda have some sympathy. When Mom Butler's family tek you outta yuh poor house an' give you the land, you nevah did know seh it did tek 'way from my people how much years ago."

"You a fool, Johnson. How much time me haffe tell you seh dem lie nah work 'pon me? Cho', you a ginal," Jim said in a softer, more cynical voice.

"Lie? Mom know ah truth me ah tell. You know how long

we ah fight fe dis land wha' Mom Butler mammy an' daddy did teef from my people? The whole parish know it, but dem scorn we an' nah tell the truth."

"Johnson," Jim began, "you have hard ears. You see like how you ah gwan nuh..." He paused, shifting his weight to another leg. "My heart ah sink go down ah me foot bottom, but me nuh care, me nuh care 'bout yuh business an' fe the hundred ah pickney you have pack up inna dat deh yard," Jim smiled, he knew he had hit below the belt, and he knew that was guaranteed to rile his adversaries.

"You dyam outta order, Butler." Kai, the normally quiet Johnson brother responded, pushing himself to the front of the argument.

"Me know, but you ugly same way," Jim replied, turning up his nose scornfully. "Me agree dat is about time you tek yuh dutty self an' wash yuh mouth, especially when you find yuhself ah fe me door."

Kai's dark face turned sour and his hands curled up into fists. Suddenly, he lunged towards Jim but his target stepped back, just out of reach. Robert stepped in, holding his brother's arm and pulling him back.

"Nuh now, Kai," Robert muttered in his ear, pushing him back. "You nevah haffe seh dat, Butler, we only ah try fe get wha' we feel is ours."

"Cho'!" Jim scoffed and spat provocatively in the Johnsons' direction.

Ivan, who had been relatively quiet up until then, leapt forward and shoved himself directly in front of Jim, his rough, unshaven face trickling with sweat, his nostrils flaring.

"You ah get outta hand now. You bettah sell we the land or else somet'ing bad might happen to you."

Ella, who had slowly worked her way into the living room,

38

breathed in sharply. What were they saying? How could they just come and start threatening her father? They couldn't. Her father's cryptic remark earlier on came back to her. Slowly she was piecing together all the elements of the big secret. But she didn't have time to come to a conclusion before her father shoved Ivan with so much force that he reeled backwards into Kai and Robert and all three Johnson brothers landed heavily on the ground, visibly shaken. They soon recovered though, and struggled to get back on their feet.

"...An' stay out!" shouted Jim, ready to close the door on the three men, but before he could do so Ivan had leapt to his feet and rushed him, his large bulk crashing forward and sending Jim flying backwards into his own house. He cried out. Mom Butler, who had also been knocked down in the attack, groaned in pain. Ella screamed at the Butler men: "Get out! Get out! Get out!" Then she herself ran out through the back door into the yard calling for her brother.

Jim had recovered sufficiently to throw Ivan off him and was about to pick himself off the floor when Kai came rushing in, punching him hard in the face. Jim fell back to the floor with a crash. A slight wound appeared above his eye which trickled blood. Kai's hand had suffered from the punch also and he held it back as his boot let rip into Jim's stomach. Ivan stood up and joined in as Jim tried to roll out of the way of the oncoming barrage.

Seething with anger, Mom Butler had picked herself up off the floor and hurled her bulk at the two men. She caught Kai squarely on the chin and blood immediately coloured his teeth. He stopped punishing Jim on the floor and was about to let fly on Mom Butler when Bill, running in from the back yard, smashed into him, flattening him against the far wall.

Robert, who had been rooted to the spot in shock up to

39

now, decided to make his move. But instead of going to his brothers' aid, he rushed into the Butlers' hallway and hauled Ivan off Jim and pushed Kai back outside the house. The two men, vexed at their brother's intrusion, cursed him and then the Butlers before slowly wandering off. Ivan, the last to leave, simply shook his head and warned "remember wha' me did ah seh," before following his brothers back to their yard.

Mom Butler, still trying to catch her breath, nodded at Bill, with a grateful look. If it hadn't been for him she would probably be in as bad a state as Jim now.

Ella helped her father to his feet. He was bloody and doubled over in pain.

"Jus' over deh so," he groaned, pointing to the rocking chair in the living room. The fight seemed to have sobered him, yet he longed for some rum to dull the pain of his suffering.

"You feel seh somet'ing bruk?" Mom Butler asked anxiously.

"Jus' bruise," Jim groaned, holding his stomach. "An' me jus' start feel sorry fe dem Johnsons..."

Though Ella was concerned for her father's well-being, she was also sulky after finally discovering the 'big secret'. Why hadn't she been told what it was all about?

"Because it's big people's business," Bill tried to hush his sister. But Ella wasn't letting it rest. She turned to her father.

"Is not fair, Dada..."

"Wha's not fair child?"

"Is not fair fe hide the truth from me. Syd Johnson ah go 'round chatting all over school. How you expect me nuh fe know? At least if I know wha' ah gwan, I can deal with it bettah."

"You too young, child, an' dat's all me want fe seh 'bout it," Mom Butler interjected.

40

Jim looked at his daughter with sympathetic eyes. To him, Ella was no longer a child. Perhaps they had been a little over-protective of her. There was no reason why she shouldn't know about the family feud which began long before she was born. But at the same time he hadn't wanted to frighten her with all the Johnsons' threats. He sighed: "Okay, you want to know wha' ah gwan?"

Ella nodded eagerly. Mom Butler folded her arms impatiently.

"A'right," Jim continued, "we sort ah rent some land to the Johnsons true dem want fe build a small house an' farm a lickle land. Me mean, we lease dem the land fe ten years an' it soon run out."

"You mean dem will be homeless, with all dem deh pickney living there an' t'ing?" Ella asked.

Jim shifted uneasily. "No, ah nuh so. Me offer fe extend dem lease, so dem won't be homeless."

"So wha'ppen then?"

"It not as simple as dat. You see, the Johnsons want fe buy the land. Dem want somet'ing dat's ours. Somet'ing dat's been in we family fe generations, you understand? An' dem claiming dat we teef the land from dem gran'dada. Nuh only dat," Jim whispered conspiratorially, "dem want more land so dat dem can build ah extension on the house an' farm more land. Dem seh dat dem ah go work science 'pon we if me nuh agree."

Mom Butler had heard enough and chastised Jim. "Cho', how you love chat so much? An' why you want frighten the child with all this foolishness 'bout 'science'? If dem foolish Johnson's wan' fe use bad obeah pon us, it will come back on dem. Mek me deal with dat cut," she said, motioning Ella away as she pressed a damp cloth saturated with antiseptic onto the

41

wound on her husband's eyebrow. He winced with pain.

"Dyam!" he cried. "Dat blasted hurt!"

Mom looked at him and kissed her teeth.

It wasn't the first time that she'd had to nurse him and it probably wouldn't be the last. It was one of the rituals of being married to a man who allowed his rum to do his talking for him. It was also the only form of affection that she showed Jim in front of the kids. Well, since Jakie's death anyway. At times like these, Bill and Ella were reminded that beneath her hard exterior, Mom Butler really loved their father as she did them. She just found it hard to show it.

"Wha' you ah go do 'bout the Johnsons, Dada?" Bill asked, a concerned look on his face.

Jim turned to the son he had considered disciplining earlier. Now his judgment was not sodden with alcohol, he felt an immense pride in his son. When the going got tough, Bill was right there by his side defending his honour, as a good son ought to.

"Wha' you feel me should do, Bill?" Jim asked.

He knew that his son didn't find it easy talking to him, and he didn't want to make him feel any more discomfort.

"Me nuh know," Bill said, shrugging his broad shoulders. "Maybe you should compromise." He lowered his voice. The word 'compromise' wasn't in his father's vocabulary.

"Compromise?" Jim shouted, then groaned as his aching side tweaked with pain. "You can't compromise with dem deh people. As soon as you give in, dem want more an' more. You allow dem an' dem will move even more ah dem dyam family yah, an' tek every dyam t'ing over." Jim looked up and caught the disappointment etched on Bill's face. He looked away. This was something in which he wasn't prepared to give an inch.

"We can't compromise, Bill," Mom interrupted. "We can't

sell wha' deh inna we family fe generations. We ah try fe preserve we history. An' besides, everyone need somewhere fe call dem own."

"Ah jus' so, Mom," Bill agreed. "The Johnsons waan somewhere fe call dem own too."

"Yes, me understand yuh point, Bill, but is not theirs in the first place. We nah throw dem out. The new lease will give dem 'nuff security but me can't give up land, 'cause people waan fe mek good off my back." Mom Butler had said her final word on the matter and went through into the kitchen to get the broom.

Bill turned to his father glumly. "You nuh understan'. We suffer too, especially El. Every time we go out an' we meet the Johnsons, dem bound fe seh somet'ing. Me jus' feel dat one day, bwoy…"

"An' me 'fraid fe the obeah!" Ella blurted out suddenly. For the first time, Bill and Jim noticed that she was trembling and that her head was wet with sweat.

"You see what happen?" Bill turned to his father.

Jim threw a reassuring arm around his daughter. "Nuh min' yaar, me dear, dem can't work science. An' anyway, we can work science back 'pon dem too, y'know."

"But meanwhile," Bill countered, "how we ah go defend we self?"

"Well," Jim began, "me can't tell unuh nah fe defend yuhself, but nuh bother get yuhself inna trouble true dem deh fool."

"Move yuh foot!" Mom barked, righting overturned furniture and sweeping up the glass from a broken framed photograph which had smashed in the struggle with the Johnsons. Suddenly, the front door swung open and slammed against the wall. Bill, thinking the Johnson's had returned,

turned with his fists up ready for another fight, and Jim struggled to his feet. It wasn't the Johnsons however, but an agitated PickneyDaddy who stepped into the room.

"Blood ah go run!" he declared, unaware of the recent events. "Your two pickney dem jus' get me mad an' upset, y'know." He waited for a response from the people in the room. Then he noticed the furniture in a state of disarray. "So what happen?" he asked. Still there was no answer. As far as Jim and Mom Butler were concerned, it was a domestic dispute, there was no need to tell the whole of Jamaica. Bill and Ella didn't say a word either. PickneyDaddy could see that he was unwelcome. He turned to go, kissing his teeth and slamming the door behind him.

Ella giggled to herself and could see a sigh of relief light up on Bill's face. Mom Butler disappeared back into the kitchen.

"Me waan some food!" Jim called out. The way he saw things, he had done his part to defend his household and this gave him certain privileges.

"Food?" Mom Butler called back. "Cock nuh know fe watch chicken, but him know fe nyam corn." A loud kiss of her teeth followed. She had just been knocked to the ground by the Johnsons and all her husband could think about was food. The rules of the house were clear, if you weren't at home on time for dinner, you went and fixed your own meal. Fortunately for Jim, his wife's heart had softened in the last few minutes and she soon re-appeared carrying some breadfruit and chicken, settling them on a nearby table. Bill and Ella took their father's arm and helped him up, carefully walking him across the room and easing him into a seat.

"You can't go ah work like dat, Dada," Bill said, reaching to pluck some breadfruit from a bowl.

"Me will sleep the pain out. Is only some bruises," Jim

replied, surprised at Bill's concern.

"Bruises?" Mom Butler laughed. "Dem mash you up good. Next time you fe 'member nuh fe cuss big man 'til yuh sure seh you done grow, 'cause you get mash up."

"Mash me?" Jim repeated in mock horror. "Ah wha' you ah deal wid? Dem nevah mash not'n. You see me, me nevah even get one proper lick from dem man deh, y'hear?"

Bill picked up on the joke and laughed. "Dada, you get mash up fe real…"

Ella felt happier than she had for weeks. Her family were together laughing and joking just like they used to. Her father's minor injuries were a small price to pay for bringing the family closer together. But, despite the fact that her mother and father weren't arguing for a change, she still felt uneasy and at the back of her mind she knew things wouldn't stay peaceful for long.

THREE
School Days

Ella was restless for most of the night lying in a pool of cold sweat. In her nightmare she was running deep from a shadow, she couldn't make out whether it was human or animal, running through the bush as fast as her legs could carry her. When she felt out of breath and about to faint, suddenly she found herself in a ring of fire, surrounded by a circle of flame that was closing in on her...

Ella jumped out of her sleep and sat up on the bed. Her throat felt dry, her stomach tight with fear. Around her, everything seemed quiet. Taking one deep breath to steady herself, she climbed out of bed and made her way to the water pipe at the back of the house. With the high moon over the peaceful night, the coconut palms cast their shadows over the yard. The water was cool and soothing, like a caress to her skin. Ella rinsed her mouth and took a gulp before turning off the tap. Somewhere down in the gully a dog barked, then a distant answer rose from somewhere even further. Ella went back inside, dried her face and hands with her flannel before returning to lay down.

Bill had stirred early, woken up by the noise of his father clattering around the house. Jim Butler had decided to go to work after all. Bill had remained in bed a while longer, lying still and listening and wondering if the truce between himself and his father would last and if they would continue being a happy family as they had been last night, or if they would revert to the confrontational relationship which had kept them apart for a year now. But he couldn't be sure and as he didn't want to start the day with an argument, he had waited until Jim departed before rising.

On hearing the front door slam, he rushed to the bedroom window and watched his father's outline disappearing down the road. Jim was limping slightly, but there seemed to be no great physical damage.

"Wha' you ah do?" Ella's voice came suddenly.

"Ah, El," her brother sighed tiredly. "You ah wake?"

"Wha' you ah do?" Ella repeated, rubbing the sleep from her eyes as she walked up to the window, her plaited hair pointing upwards as if she had been petrified by something in her dreams.

"Not'n. Me jus' ah watch Dada go to work," Bill said.

"Him a'right?" Ella asked, yawning.

"Yeah, him seem to be," Bill said. "Me nevah speak to him. Him gone through the door before me get up."

"Wha' the time, Bill?" she stretched.

"Me nuh know," Bill crowed, looking at the space on his wrist where a watch would have been if his parents could afford one for him. "Mussi 'bout six o'clock."

"Can't be dat late," Ella responded. "Dada always leave the yard by five-thirty."

"You right," Mom Butler's voice boomed as she opened the

47

bedroom door and entered. "Dat dyam fool-man tek up him sick self an' fly ah work. Even though him still feel mash up. Like fire deh ah mus-mus tail him t'ink ah cool breeze." Mom Butler's face creased with a mix of pain and impatience. "Quarter past six," she said finally, before leaving her children and making her way out the back to the standpipe for her morning freshness. Ella exchanged glances with her brother, yawned again, and floated back into bed.

"Me ah lie down fe a while," she said.

"Nuh fall asleep," Bill said, "ah school today."

Ella did fall asleep and didn't she know it. She was there again in another nightmare, on the periphery of the action this time. The scene was vivid: there was a fire burning with about eight children around it, and a tiny man beside them. The man's head was wrapped in a bright red turban which dangled close to the fire. He was mumbling something incomprehensible and spinning around and twirling his head as if some demon had possessed his soul. Ella could feel her heart beating faster and faster and she became increasingly aware that she didn't want to be in the dream any longer. She could feel herself trying to outrun the nightmare, trying to wake up, but to no avail.

The man persisted with his chanting and produced a bottle, the contents of which he emptied over the raging fire, causing an explosion of flames which engulfed the children. As she stared in the flames, Ella noticed someone rising up from the middle of the fire. She gasped as she made out the figure of a small boy, screaming in pain as the flames burned his flesh. The man lifted his head and let out an ear-piercing laugh. The little boy turned to Ella in her hiding place and called out, "Ella, help me!" It was only then that she recognized the boy.

"Little Jakie!" she screamed. But it was too late. The boy was consumed by the flames and fell back into the pit of fire from whence he came. By then the scene had become a blur and Ella began to slip slowly out of her sleep.

When Bill shoved her for the third time, she responded slowly with a deep sigh. Now that she was awake, no nightmares could trouble her.

"You haffe do dat?" she growled, her eyes open wide.

"Yes," Bill responded. "You know the time?" There was no answer. "Half past! Dat ah the time an' you bettah shift yuhself before Mom ketch you sleeping."

Startled into action by those last lingering words, Ella shot up and, before Bill could speak again, was out the back door on her way to the standpipe for a quick wash.

When she got back to the house dripping wet, her mother was waiting for her.

"How much time me must tell you fe dry off yuhself properly before you come back inna the house?" she roared.

"Me soon dry, Mom," Ella said, trying to towel herself and pull on her clothes at the same time.

Mom Butler sent a swift slap across her head. "Maybe you will start listening now," she said before heading towards the kitchen muttering something about, "Last pickney always kill mumma..."

Ella was stunned by the unexpected blow but held back the tears which threatened to fall as she pulled on her flowery dress and her simple sandals which had long faded from their original white colour.

"You see, El," Bill said, "you jus' nah listen to me when me tell you t'ings fe yuh own good."

"Bill," Ella said, then paused. Bill looked at his sister. "Move an' go 'way!"

Ella's blood was boiling from the sting of Mom Butler's

slap. Her mouth opened again to launch a further attack on her brother, but suddenly their mother appeared at the bedroom door again.

"You mean fe tell me seh you nah move yet?" Mom Butler yelled, blocking the entrance of the door. Ella snatched up her satchel and stood to attention.

"Mom," she began, "me ready. Can I have me food money please?"

It was quick thinking on Ella's part to distract her mother that way and Mom Butler went off to her room to get the money.

"Gal, yuh fast," Bill chuckled as they left the house and began the journey to school.

"Bwoy, me couldn't bother get another slap like dat deh one Mom jus' give me. Me ears-root ah burn."

Bill nodded but seemed distant. His thoughts were elsewhere.

"Wha' wrong?" Ella asked. "Gwan, tell me nuh."

Bill pushed his hands deep in his pockets and hunched his shoulders.

"Not'n," he said, silently kicking up some turf. Then he added, "Me jus' vex' 'bout all the obeah business."

"You t'ink the Johnson's can work science fe true?"

Bill shrugged his shoulders. How could he know? All he was sure of was that obeah was evil and the word made him go cold inside. No amount of land was worth any evil befalling their family. Bill pondered his thoughts for a moment longer, then he remembered himself and how frightened Ella had been by the very mention of obeah last night. "But nuh worry yuhself. Nuh dem alone can work science, y'know. An' you have me an' Dada to protect you." He tried to laugh it off, but Ella wasn't convinced.

"Me dream Little Jakie, y'know," Ella confessed, as she strolled along. She didn't get a response from Bill who merely stared at the road up ahead.

"You nevah hear wha' me did seh?"

"Yeah, me hear you," Bill acknowledged, "but me nuh waan talk 'bout Little Jakie."

Bill was firm. As far as he was concerned, that was the end of the matter. Ella decided not to pursue it. For now anyway.

"Watch yah nuh," Ella said. They had reached the bend in the road in front of Ole Miller's house. "You see wha' me see?" she asked in an alarmed voice.

"No," Bill answered, trying hard to avoid staring directly at the ramshackle old house.

"Me t'ink Ole Miller escape," Ella whispered, quickening her pace.

"Why you seh dat?" Bill questioned.

"The gate," Ella announced. "It's open."

It was as if all else became unimportant. Bill's eyes zoomed in on the house and focused on the gate that was, for the first time, flung wide open.

"Me nuh believe it, El," Bill said, looking nervously around. "Ole Miller nah come out a dyam."

"Me nuh waan find out an' get nyam alive," Ella said, running away.

Ella disappeared up the road with effortless ease. When she looked back, she saw Bill struggling to catch up.

Ella was waiting on the bridge at Roaring River. "Why you have to run so fast?" Bill said, trotting across the bridge. "You mustn't carry on do dat," he warned. "Ole Miller can be anywhere, jus' ah wait fe you fe run inna him arms."

"Forget dat," Ella laughed, "me too quick."

They continued the rest of the walk to school in silence, Bill waiting for his sister to apologise and Ella believing she had nothing to apologise about.

When they reached the school gate twenty minutes later the school bell hadn't been rung yet and the school children were still running around outside.

"How yuh poppa?" a cheeky voice squeaked from behind them.

Bill rolled his eyes up and he turned slowly. "Syd," he began, staring annoyed into the intruder's face, "you nuh have not'n fe do?" A muscle high up on Bill's cheekbone began to dance.

"No, me nuh have not'n, you ah go give me somet'ing bettah fe do?"

"You waan trouble?" Bill asked tentatively, as he eyed Syd Johnson's friends closing in on the action. Syd didn't answer.

"You bettah galang, El," Bill said quietly to Ella, keeping one eye on the gathering crowd.

"Naa!" Ella refused, brushing her brother's arm away in defiance. If Syd wanted trouble, she was going to stand firm right next to her brother. She wasn't running anywhere.

"Ella," Bill shouted, "nuh act like no hero."

For a moment Ella wondered if her brother truly believed she was just trying to be brave. It wasn't about that at all. She might not be strong, she considered, but at least she could help Bill as her mother had helped Dada in the confrontation with the Johnsons the previous night.

"Wha' ah gwan yah?" the voice of Mr Brown, loud and threatening, breached the uneasy quiet. No sooner had he arrived, than the crowd dispersed and left Ella and Bill squaring up to an invisible enemy.

"Wha' ah gwan?" Mr Brown repeated, this time louder and sterner. His voice carried around the playground.

"Me nuh know," Bill answered somewhat bemused.

"Wha' you mean, you nuh know?" Mr Brown asked pointedly, peering at Bill through thick glasses.

"Well," Bill began, "Syd Johnson an' him friend dem start gwan like dem waan fight we."

"Don't be absurd, bwoy," Mr Brown said dismissively. "Dat sort ah t'ing doesn't happen in this school...woe betide any unruly pupil me ketch. Nuh let me see unuh in anymore trouble fe the day." With that, Mr Brown rang the bell for the commencement of the day's schooling.

"Nuh get involved with Syd Johnson, Bill," Ella pleaded as they parted to go to their respective classes.

The door of Ella's classroom slammed shut and she was snatched back to reality. She had been deep in thought, still concerned about what the Johnsons were going to do next. Their threats echoed in her mind and the continuing hostility with Syd Johnson was becoming wearisome. Syd she could deal with but the thought of her family being in danger worried her deeply.

Mr Brown was in an impatient mood and had no time for any slackness in his class today. When he had first arrived in the parish from Kingston, he had been a cheerful and popular teacher with modern ideas about teaching and a belief that his pupils could be disciplined without corporal punishment. But the sudden death of his wife had changed him and he was now often moody and seemed, on the whole, to be less committed to his students' education.

He shuffled across to his large imposing pulpit and stood in front of the seventeen or so children who made up his class.

"Me will tek the register now," he barked, flicking over the front cover of the register. "Anderson?"

"Yes, Sir," Ruth Anderson replied in a croaky voice.

"Arnold?" Mr Brown continued; a muffled reply came back...

The roll call was completed without incident.

"Two absent," Mr Brown declared, searching the faces of the children in the class for an answer. No acceptable excuses were forthcoming for Bubsy Walker and Jacqueline Evans. Ella looked across at Mavis John who looked back at her and sniggered. They knew like everyone else in the room that the two were playing truant. Mr Brown suspected it also.

"Before me start the lesson," Mr Brown began, "me jus' waan fe mek sure everyone remember the big event happening nex' week." He looked around at the multitude and saw blank faces staring back at him. "But wait, me remind you ah dis only a few weeks ago."

Some members of the class nodded, Ella included. The rest of the children waited for Mr Brown to continue.

"Nex' week," he said, "is sports day. Yes, it deh yah again; but this time with a difference." Mr Brown looked at his class and smiled smugly. "This year we have ah invitation race at the end of the day, where anyone from any class can enter."

The class gasped. Never before had there been an opportunity for the younger members of the school to pit their athletic talents against the older ones. It seemed like a direct challenge to Ella, for the whole class knew that she would find irresistible the opportunity to race against the likes of Skully McLean and Junior Tucker. These two older boys were well known across the parish for their running abilities and it was no secret that Ella longed to race them, though they had always scoffed at her requests.

"So," Mr Brown asked, his eyes scanning the pupils in his

class, "any questions?"

Ella's arm shot up immediately.

"Yes, Ella."

"How far will the race be please, Sir?" she asked excitedly. Already she could feel butterflies of excitement in her stomach, this was her big chance and she was keen to find out as much as she could in advance.

"It will be jus' over four miles."

Ella beamed from ear to ear and sat back in her wooden chair. Four miles was a distance she would relish.

"Me tek it then, Ella Louis, dat you will be competing inna the race?"

"Me t'ink so," Ella acknowledged. "But the competition ah go strong."

"Yes, me know," Mr Brown nodded understandingly. "But, not'n ventured, not'n gained."

That was enough chit-chat with his favourite student, Mr Brown decided, and told the class to open their Jamaican history books and turn to the chapter on The *White Witch of Rose Hall*. Meanwhile, he had to attend an important staff meeting. His parting words suggested he had little faith in his students behaving in his absence. "Me ah go test unuh 'pon the story later so unuh bettah read it until me come back."

The class erupted as soon as Mr Brown disappeared. Ruth Anderson's exercise book went flying across the room. The bully of the class, Boisy Jones, let out a deep bellied laugh at his own antics.

"Yuh ah eediat, Boisy," Ruth Anderson shouted as she scrambled to pick up the book.

"Is who yuh ah call eediat?" Boisy questioned, his features darkening.

"Yuh is t'ick as well as ugly?" Ruth Anderson blurted out,

unafraid of the bully.

"Cho," Boisy brushed the comment aside, "me can't bother wid yuh." He turned to his friends and giggled.

Meanwhile, Ella kept her head down to read the task Mr Brown had set them, a volley of screwed up pieces of paper flying over her head in the direction of Jeffrey Arnold.

"Is who do dat?" he cried out, jumping to his feet. By this time, Boisy's attention was already distracted in the task of taxing some unfortunate boy of his lunch money. "Is mussi you, Thomas; is always you. Yuh coming like leech."

Jeffrey Arnold hated Boisy. For that matter everybody hated Boisy. But Jeffrey *really* hated him, having been beaten up by the bully and his friends not too long ago. Boisy didn't fancy taking Jeffrey on on his own.

Ella's face screwed up. She was actually trying to concentrate on what she was meant to be doing. But it was impossible with all the commotion.

"Is not worth it," Ella said, trying to talk Jeffrey out of the developing situation.

"Yeah," Jeffrey acknowledged, quenching the fire in his eyes, "the bwoy nuh worth it fe true." He sighed deeply and left the situation hanging for another time.

"Look 'pon you," Loran Douglas teased Ella.

"Yeah?" Ella replied.

"Yuh too smart," Loran persisted.

"Cho!" Ella dismissed her, "is wha' ah bother you?"

"Yuh too stuck 'pon the teacher dem. Coming like you love dem aarf," Loran said, with a wicked grin on her face.

"Is wha' yuh ah seh?" Ella asked.

"Me nah seh not'n, but you up inna dem too much."

Ella looked puzzled, unable to catch Loran's drift.

"Maybe if you did have enough sense, Loran, and do some

work instead of minding my business, dem would ah like you too."

The disruption of the class continued with some of the pupils seemingly drunk with misbehaviour. Mr Brown's absence was too good an opportunity to waste on reading history. It all changed when the teacher suddenly appeared at the door, just in time to catch the paper missile which Boisy Jones had launched across the classroom towards the back of a classmate's head.

Mr Brown beckoned Boisy to the front of the room. The boy knew he was in for it and walked as slowly as his legs could carry him. Mr Brown also took his time in twisting the disrespectful pickney's ear until Boisy was standing on tiptoe howling with pain. The burning sensation would only last an hour or two, but the memory of this pain would be uppermost in Boisy's mind the next time he decided to misbehave in Mr Brown's class.

Ella was among the handful of pupils excused from the classroom when the lunch time bell rang but, alas, for those who were bold enough to ignore Mr Brown's orders, it would be a lunch time spent reading *The White Witch of Rose Hall* chapter in their Jamaican history books, under the watchful eye of their teacher.

Bill was already waiting at the gate for his sister at the end of school later that afternoon.

"Whe' you did deh?" he questioned her. "You know yuh haffe careful with dem idiot bwoy dem around."

They made their way homewards at a steady pace.

"You ah go run inna the race?"

"Try an' stop me," Ella replied confidently. "Nobody

believe a small gal can beat the older boys an' me nuh even know meself if me stand a chance. But me going enjoy meself."

Indeed, Ella was so looking forward to taking part in the race that she feared she would think of little else in the next few days.

"Me bet money 'pon yuh, y'know..."

They hadn't walked far when they came across an old woman, her legs so bowed that Ella feared she might fall over with every step.

"Bwoy," Ella began, as she felt her leg joints, "the woman leg dem ben' bad," she giggled.

"Howdy," came a voice that shot past them. It was Pastor Stephenson on his way to exorcise the faithful of unholy spirits. He was late, typically, and blazed a trail despite his age.

"Bwoy," Bill observed, "some people jus' love fe rush, dat's why dem always late."

Ella nodded in agreement.

Just then a trio of men appeared out of the bush up ahead, brandishing machetes which gleamed menacingly in the sunlight.

"How yuh folks?" asked the one man who Bill recognized as one of his father's drinking friends.

"Dem a'right, sah," Bill answered.

"Tell dem Francie seh howdy," the man said before disappearing with his companions.

"Dem man did 'fraid me, yuh see," Ella admitted.

Bill said nothing, but the sudden appearance of the machete-wielding men had also made his heart thump for a moment.

Further up the track they met Mrs Jones, the mother of Ella's bullying classmate. Unlike her son, Mrs Jones was extremely pleasant and genuinely liked by most people. She was known by everyone for being able to balance up to four baskets on her head at the same time, while most people could only manage one. On seeing the Butler siblings Mrs Jones reached into one of the fruit baskets above her head and handed them each a juicy soursap.

As they continued on their journey, they could just make out the figure of the 'White Woman'. No-one would admit to knowing this woman who, regardless of the day or weather, always wore white and was completely that colour from head to toe. "But she nuh white like white smaddy, Bill?" Ella asked.

"No, she nuh white, she a black woman. But she bleach up and paint up her skin and wear white wig, scarf and clothes. All the shoes she wear 'pon her foot, white also."

The puzzled look on Ella's face said that she failed to understand how any woman would choose to do such a thing. The word was that obeah had made her turn that way, Bill said. And truly, it was difficult for Ella to come up with a better explanation.

The rest of their journey home was uneventful. They joked with each other and talked about school, the Johnsons and the big fight from the night before. As they approached the Ole Miller house, neither of them noticed a figure crouched in the bushes outside.

"Blood ah go run," a croaky voice rasped, as a pair of hands grabbed the two siblings by the scruff of their necks. Ella screamed for help and only just managed to wriggle free and sprint down the road screaming for 'Mumma' to tell her that 'Ole Miller escape and try nyam Bill'.

Bill, meanwhile, was thrown into a nearby bush. He too was terrified and let out a scream for mercy despite himself.

"Ah-ahhh!" PickneyDaddy's voice laughed. "Is only me."

Ella slowed down and turned her head.

59

"Ah you, PickneyDaddy?" she quipped nervously, turning to face him.

PickneyDaddy fell to the ground laughing. "Yes, m'dear," he replied, "me did tell you seh me would ah get you back from the other day," he scoffed.

"Dat wasn't funny, you ole dawg," Ella said. "Me did feel ah Ole Miller come fe nyam me flesh."

"Bwoy, you nuh fe do dem t'ings, PickneyDaddy," Bill said, dusting himself down.

"But of course me must," PickneyDaddy sniggered. "You 'member wha' you did to me wehday? Or you feel me forget?" He looked at the both of them as they regained their composure.

"You nuh see seh a pure accident when Ella spit inna yuh face," Bill insisted.

PickneyDaddy pulled the two children towards him and wrapped his arms around them affectionately. "You 'member the ole dawg dat did live ah yonder?" He pointed to the bush to his left.

"Wha' dawg you ah talk 'bout?"

"The dawg with the one foot. Every time you see him, him foot cock up and him ah hop like so…" PickneyDaddy did his best to imitate the dog. Bill and Ella giggled at the sight of a grown man hopping on one leg with his other leg cocked. They knew they were in for one of PickneyDaddy's infamous tall tales.

"Yeah, me 'member dat deh one-foot dawg," Bill said.

"Hee-hee, me know you would ah 'member the dawg me ah talk. Yuh see…" PickneyDaddy paused. "Yuh see before it lose it leg the dawg did bad nuh yaars an' me know dat one day somet'ing mus' haffe happen to him. Everyday the dyam dawg line up ah the school gate an' wait till the children fe

60

come out. When the pickney dem come out ah school, the dyam dawg would ah rush dem an' chase dem down ah the road an' all ah bite dem ankle an' foot, like it nuh nyam food fe days an' all weeks.

"One day one ah the pickney faada did go to the school an' when him ah lef' wid the lickle gal, the dawg nah chase dem off an' somehow dem end up inna bush. From dat day deh, the dawg disappear an' nobody could see the sint'ing fe months.

"Well, after a few months the dawg come back, but it nuh lose one of it back leg. The dawg haffe walk wid one of him leg cock up inna the air like it ah go peepee.

"Someone seh dat the man who the dawg chase was one obeah man an' him blood did poison the dawg when it bite him an' it fall down ah sleep. Then the man jus' chop off the leg an' up till now him have it an' ah walk up an' down ah Honeyhole, with it 'pon him belt, fe show the other dawg dem nah fe trouble him neither him pickney dem.

"When the school pickney dem see seh the dawg sick an' ah hobble 'pon t'ree foot, dem start punish the dawg yuh see. Anywhere you see the dawg, pickney ah t'row stone after it, an' all ah tek up stick ah lick it an' the dawg couldn't even run fe get 'way.

"One day the same lickle gal ah chase the dawg an' she fall down one pit dem workman did dig an' lef', true dem lazy. When the dawg see dat, it jus' turn 'round, cock him foot an' wet her up wid him peepee."

PickneyDaddy finished his story with a satisfied grin on his face, but Ella and Bill's perplexed expressions told him that he had omitted the point of the story.

"Dat fe show unuh seh, every dawg have him day."

"So, what happen to the dawg after?" Ella queried.

"Bwoy, me nuh know, y'know sah, but me hear seh most ah

the obeah man in Honeyhole did eat some dawg meat dat night deh," PickneyDaddy concluded, licking his lips.

Ella looked horrified. PickneyDaddy smiled mischievously.

FOUR
Murder at the Cane & Tobacco Farm

The Butler kids arrived at the front door of their house simultaneously, neither of them triumphing in that eternal race to see who could get home first. They called out their familiar greeting to their mother who was in the kitchen, preparing their meal. She turned her head slightly to acknowledge them, before returning to the work at hand. Ella glanced over at her mother affectionately. Mom Butler never seemed to stop working. In a way, Ella was proud of how hard-working she was but, at the same time, she wished she and her mother had more time to be together.

After changing quickly from their school uniform to their domestic clothes, Bill and Ella went about their chores. Every day after they came home from school, housework awaited them. Each knew their tasks and went about them without fuss or fight. Ella didn't need to be reminded of her duties, for there was usually a pile of ackees waiting for her to shell in the backyard. And if it wasn't ackee, it was yams waiting to be peeled. And if it wasn't that, it was feeding the chickens that roamed freely in the backyard. There was always something waiting for Ella to do when she came home from school, Mom Butler made sure of that.

Bill was soon outside in the yard too, swinging a machete above his head and bringing it down swiftly to divide the logs in two. He had become something of an expert in chopping firewood. In fact, he didn't see it as a chore at all but as an afternoon workout to develop his youthful arm muscles. Sometimes he would chop more wood than the family could use in a week and Mom Butler would have to find him some less masculine chores to be getting on with.

The sun had long disappeared when Mom Butler finally gave up on Jim and started to serve the evening meal without waiting for him to come home. The meal was much the same as the previous night, yam and banana, as Mom Butler usually cooked enough food for two days, but today Ella just didn't feel hungry. There was a tenseness in her stomach, whether from nerves or otherwise. She was excited about the forthcoming race, but that alone could not have resulted in her loss of appetite.

Bill, on the other hand, had a voracious appetite and wolfed down his dinner in minutes. He had been reflecting heavily on the events of the night before. His relationship with his father had been strained and awkward for some time but last night proved how close they could be, even if it was due to a fight. Dada, for all his faults, was not as bad as he wanted people to believe. But there was no time for differences between them now that they were up against the Johnsons. And Bill reminded himself over and over again that whatever else happened, 'blood is t'icker than water'.

His thoughts were interrupted by a loud knock on the door. Startled, Mom Butler hurried across to answer it.

Butler?" A policeman stood at the door staring at

at is it?" Mom Butler asked, looking deeply
ery rarely did a policeman venture to remote parts
such as their home, and then only to deliver bad
thing awful must have happened and it had to
.. He was the only member of the family not at
Johnsons' threat echoed in her mind and for a brief
.er life with Jim flashed before her eyes, like a high-
.lage of the good times and the bad times. In that same
., she made a silent pact with God that she would do
ng, if only no harm had come to Jim. Then she breathed
.rply, expecting the worst.

'You did hear wha' me seh, Mrs Butler?" the policeman
ked, stepping closer. He had been trying to explain the
purpose of his visit, but it seemed like she was in a trance.

Mom Butler focused on the officer. "Sorry, Sah," she
apologized, "wha' you did seh?" She had to pull herself
together. If it was to be the worst, she had to put on a
courageous face for the sake of the children. They would be
upset enough as it was if any harm had befallen their father.

"Me seh dat yuh husband lock up down ah Trinityville
Police Station," the policeman repeated. He watched Mom
Butler's face change slowly from concern to relief and finally to
anger as the news sunk in. Jim had been in and out of the local
police cells so many times for being drunk and disorderly that
it didn't surprise her. But why had they sent a police officer to
inform her? She would, as usual, have found out anyway in the
morning when he staggered home still unsober.

"Him deh ah jail again? Ah nuh not'n officer. Me husband
love rest ah jail house. Is hotel unuh run down deh? 'Cause it
coming like the same guests return time an' time again."

The police officer observed the woman in front of him with a bemused look. He said, "you can visit him, but not fe long. Dem have him 'pon a murder charge!"

"Ah wha'...?" Mom Butler was stunned into silence. Ella too stood with her mouth wide open and looked on in horror as the policeman confirmed his earlier statement. She didn't know what to say and could think of nothing more than that her father was in a lot of trouble. Confused, she went to her mother's side and held her hand for comfort.

"Is a'right, Mom."

But Mom Butler was deaf to her daughter's reassuring words. She was too pre-occupied with her own thoughts of doom. The policeman's words had struck her like a bolt of lightning. God seemed to have spared her husband's life with one hand and taken it away again with the other.

"Wha' murder?" she eventually asked the policeman through watery eyes.

"The murder ah Robert Johnson," the policeman replied bluntly. "Dem find him down a gully over by the Cane an' Tobacco Farm. Him did string up 'pon one tree wha' the pickney dem use fe swing."

"So how dem know is Jim do it?" Mom Butler retorted instantly.

"Well," the policeman fingered his tight shirt collar looking for, but not finding, more breathing space, "according to 'nuff people, yuh husband an' the Johnson man did ah fight last nigh an' me hear seh yuh husband did waan kill him."

Mom Butler kissed her teeth loudly. She wasn't going to stand here and listen to some idiot bwoy talking about things he knew nothing about. "Listen, you nuh know not'n. Every puppy have him flea...anyway, me nuh waan chat to you no more."

66

The policeman wasn't expecting Mom Butler to slam the door in his face and when it happened it only narrowly missed the tip of his nose. He stared at the door in front of him, then shrugged his shoulders. The woman was lucky, if his nose had been a fraction longer he would now be charging her for the very serious crime of assaulting an officer of the law. He turned and walked back to his car, the engine of which had been idling quietly in the background.

Inside the house Mom Butler turned to her children. Ella was sobbing quietly and Bill's eyes sparkled with water. Suddenly, she felt like crying also and, before she realized it, she was comforting them in a double embrace. It was a show of emotion that had taken a long time coming and the three wept together for a short while until Mom Butler regained her composure and drew away.

"Come, we haffe go an' see yuh faada," she said quietly, re-wrapping her headscarf.

The three hurried out of the house and flagged down a mini-bus which was heading towards Trinityville. The bus was packed solid with passengers and Ella, the first to board, had to squeeze between two large women whose faces were dripping with sweat and who had damp armpits. Mom Butler perched on the end of another seat and gave the old man in the front their fares. She was tired and fed up.

The bus drove for a few miles, following the winding road to the police station in the next valley. Bleating goats jumped out of the roadside as the run-down vehicle, overladen with its human cargo, roared past and smiling pedestrians, some with firewood on their heads, others standing chatting idly, answered the loud honk of the bus driver's horn with a friendly wave. To anyone else it would have seemed like they were travelling through idyllic countryside; everywhere you looked, the beauty of the Creator's plan smiled back at you. But to Ella, it was one of the most miserable journeys she had made. Her mind was confused, she didn't know what to think, but one thing was for sure, police meant trouble. Similar thoughts were going through Bill's mind, while Mom Butler simply stared ahead through the bus' wide windscreen as she considered, for the first time since she married, the possibility of life without Jim.

"One stop, driver!" Mom Butler shouted. The bus drew up almost immediately and Ella, Bill and their mother got out.

As the vehicle pulled away, they could see the jail-house across the road—a grey-coloured concrete building that was smaller than the jail-house in town. They crossed the road and stood for a moment at the bottom of the stone steps that led to the verandah of the police station. Mom Butler climbed up first, closely followed by Ella and Bill. She pushed the door to the building and it creaked open.

"Me can help you, Momma?"

Mom Butler adjusted the scarf on her head and answered the tall, slim policeman sitting with his legs hitched up on the desk as he rocked gently on the back legs of his chair. "Me come fe see Jim Butler," Mom Butler said abruptly. "One policeman tell me seh him deh yah."

The policeman studied the woman before him for a moment and then glanced at the two children with her. He was working things out in his head. It finally all made sense and he grinned wickedly.

"You did hear wha' me seh?" Mom Butler asked angrily. "Me waan fe see me husban'!" The young policeman was too discourteous for her liking. If he had known her he would have realized that Mom Butler a woman who had little patience for slack behaviour. Now, at least, he understood that she

68

meant business.

The policeman got up reluctantly. "If you come dis way me will mek you see him."

It wasn't the first time that Jim had fallen foul of the law but it was the first time Bill and Ella had seen the inside of a jail-house. Their father had on occasion been locked up overnight for disturbing the peace and a spell in the cell often gave him ample opportunity to sober up.

Once through the door they found themselves at the start of a short corridor with two heavy-duty metal doors to the right and two to the left. Mom Butler looked at the policeman, who nodded and guided them to the very last cell. He then opened the small hatch and, simultaneously, rapped loudly on the door: "Visitors for you!"

"A'right," came the croaky voice of Jim Butler. "You ah go bruk down the dyam door?"

Mom Butler smiled. Even though they had their differences, Jim was still her husband and she was glad to hear that he was in good spirits despite the murder charge. The policeman released the lock and the door creaked open.

"You have ten minutes," said the officer as he ushered the three of them into the cell.

Mom Butler stared at Jim sitting alone in the cell. He looked at her with the beginnings of a smile, but he could see in her eyes a look which summed up his helplessness. She wanted to hug him like in the old days, to make sure he was all right. But then, like all the other times she felt like this, she remembered Jakie and her feelings hardened slightly.

"You jus' ah go stan' up there?" Jim asked.

"You kill dat deh Johnson man?"

"Cho'!" Jim cried in outrage, turning his back. "Me nuh know not'n 'bout dat deh sint'ing yah."

69

Mom Butler sighed with relief. Of course her husband was innocent, she just had to be sure. Ella threw her arms around her father and squeezed him in an affectionate hug, while Bill stood back quietly watching.

"So how dem lock you up?" Mom Butler continued.

"Bwoy," Jim began, scratching his unshaven chin, "me nuh know, y'know." He paced across the small cell and patted Bill on the shoulder.

Bill looked embarrassed, hanging his head low and avoiding eye contact.

"Me did go down ah the Cane and Tobacco Farm, like me usual, an' after a few hours dem man start gwan bad true the dyam bwoy Johnson, him stop work an' gone ah gully fe somet'ing. Me did follow him, to tell him dat me nuh like how him come ah me yard an' start war, but me lef' him true him ah gwan with stupidness, an' ah taunt me 'bout wehday. So when Bigshot gone down fe get the lazy brute, Bigshot start scream an' shout an' me see him ah run an' come, like duppy did ah chase him."

Jim paused and they could hear the distant ringing of a telephone.

"Anyhow," Jim began again, turning to Mom Butler, "Bigshot couldn't talk true him breath short, but when him revive an' him blow come back him seh dat Robert Johnson dead, an' him did string up like a goat 'pon one tree." Jim sighed and slumped down onto the bed's hard mattress.

"So, how dem lock you up?" Mom Butler repeated the question that, up to now, Jim still hadn't answered.

"Two twos the police dem hol' me up, an' seh dat me go ah gully an' murder him. Bwoy, how it look?" Jim said throwing his arms in the air and jumping off the bed. "Me stupid enough fe go ah gully jus' before dem find him, an' everybody know 'bout the fight we did have."

"Me know you nevah do it," Ella cried, hugging her father even more tightly. Mom and Bill also gathered around Jim and the whole family hugged each other together, for the first time in many months. A sudden knock on the door echoed around the cell. It was the end of their visiting time.

"You could lef' we fe a few more minutes?" Mom Butler called out. She glanced at Jim and he stared back at her with a slightly puzzled expression. The door opened inwards and the policeman who had brought them to Jim's cell walked in. He had an uncertain look on his face as he wiped the sweat from his forehead with the back of his hand. He looked nervous, scared even.

"Wha'ppen?" Jim asked the policeman, his forehead creasing with concern.

The officer's eyes narrowed as they met Jim's. "Bwoy, me jus' get one call from Water Valley police station," he said agitatedly. He shifted uneasily as if searching for a way to explain what he had to say. "Dem find one nex' smaddy dead down ah the Cane & Tobacco Farm dis afternoon, string up same way like fe the Johnson man."

All eyes turned to Jim. Before the prisoner could protest his innocence, the policeman continued. "The boss seh is a more serious case dis now. Him decide seh you mussi innocent. Some police ah search the area fe clues."

Jim's eyes lit up. "You mean fe seh me can lef' dis dead-hole? Bwoy, you should well know dat me innocent from the start."

Mom Butler let out a huge sigh of relief. Ella and Bill grinned and rejoiced at the good news.

Jim stood up slowly. "Who dem find?" he asked as he ushered his children out of the cell.

"One ol' man," the policeman said coldly. "Nobody know him still. The poor bwoy nevah stan' a chance. The rope did hitch up so tight 'pon him neck, it cut right through to the bone!" The policeman looked uneasy.

The alarming revelation turned Ella's stomach.

"Oh, Mom!" she howled, reaching for her mother.

"Nevah mind yaar, if you fe dead with rope, gunshot can't tek yuh life," Mom Butler said soothingly, before wrapping an arm around her and leading her outside.

They managed to get a taxi as soon as they got outside. It was packed, as were all the taxis which ran back to Roaring River, but it was still better than walking several miles home.

Jim was silent on the journey home and Ella caught her mother studying him with a look of concern.

Twenty minutes later they arrived home. Bill, Ella and Mom Butler got out of the taxi and headed straight for the house but Jim held back and when the taxi had pulled away, he stayed by the roadside with his hands deep in his trouser pockets.

"Wha' wrong with you?" Mom Butler shouted back at him, when she realized that Jim wasn't behind her.

"Me soon come!" he called. "Me ah go 'round so fe a few minutes." And with that he headed slowly towards the Johnsons' house which was visible in the distance. As he neared he could see Robert's children Beverly and Mary playing outside. They burst into tears when they looked up and noticed Jim, and scampered swiftly into the house.

"Momma, momma," Beverly bawled, "the wicked man ah come."

When he heard that, Jim wanted to turn and walk back, but he had to go through with this. He had to let them know that he didn't kill Robert.

"Wha' you ah do yah?" came the unwelcoming voice of

Marian Johnson, a machete poised in her hand. "You nevah content fe kill me husban', you haffe come down yah fe taunt me!"

"Listen," Jim began, "me…"

"Shut yuh mout'!" Marian screamed. "How the police let you outta jail so fast? Wha' dem waan you fe go do, kill off one nex' smaddy?"

"Me nevah kill yuh husban'," Jim asserted, eyeing Marian's machete by her side

"You is ah liad an' me nuh know wha' sort ah obeah you ah work mek the police let you go widout justice fe me husban'." Marian seemed to almost choke on her tears in her blind rage. "You feel you is the only one who can work obeah? Me did seh me wouldn't fling no science 'pon you 'cause you would ah change yuh mind 'bout the lan'. But it coming like me haffe serve you ah sure."

"Is wha' you ah seh?" Jim seemed to lose his inhibitions for a moment as he considered Marian's threat. To practice obeah was one thing, but to openly admit to it was altogether more serious. And then to threaten someone with it as brazenly as Marian was doing was tantamount to suicide. In the parish of St Thomas, fools had lost their lives over such threats.

"Me know dat yuh family did ah practice dem wicked obeah from time and me did swear blind dat you nuh deh 'pon me lan' ah mix up yuh bad t'ings fe lick out people life. You better mek sure you come off me lan' wid dat deh business."

"But stop!" Marian cried alarmingly. "The man done kill off me husban' an' him so bad fe come 'pon me place an' ah shoot off him mout'. When me done wid you, yuh see, you ah go nyam dawg an' ah walk up an' down ah beg yuh pickney dem fe food."

In his anger, Jim had forgotten the whole point of his

coming over to the Johnson house. He had come in peace, to offer his condolences in light of Robert Johnson's death, not to fight. He understood also that Marian must be grief-stricken over the death of her husband and decided he should forgive and forget, despite Marian's hysterical threats of obeah.

"Marian, me nevah kill yuh husban'!" he re-asserted.

"Don't chat foolishness, Butler, you do it yes, an' you ah go pay wid yuh life." Marian grinned as a different mood suddenly washed over her.

"No, Marian, you must listen," Jim pleaded, holding his arms out in front of him and backing off. "You nevah hear seh dem find one nex' body down ah the Cane & Tobacco Farm an' the killing did gwan when me did deh inna the prison."

Marian stood back for a few seconds, seemingly shocked by this latest piece of information. Her arm dropped to her side, and the machete dug into the ground.

"Wha' ah gwan?" Kai Johnson said, stepping out of the house to see what all the commotion was about, a machete hanging loosely from his waist belt. "Oh, is you…"

At the same time, Ivan came from the side of the house carrying a machete.

"Hold on," Jim interjected, "unuh nevah hear wha' did 'appen down ah the Cane & Tobacco Farm after dem arrest me?"

"Ah wha' the heck you ah talk seh, Butler?" Kai bellowed. "Wha' mek you so bad? You can't come yah so bold, an' feel seh not'n nah go 'appen to you."

"Me come fe tell you seh dat me nevah kill Robert; is smaddy else do it," Jim stuttered as sweat began to gather on his forehead.

"Ha!" Ivan gave a deep-throated dismissal of Jim's claims and began his bloodthirsty advance, machete at the ready.

"Listen," Jim began again, the authority in his voice slipping away with every word, "dat is why dem release me so soon. Dem find a nex' body down there an' the police know seh I don't have not'n to do with them killing business."

"Shut yuh mout'!" Marian screamed, brandishing her machete. "Is you do it, so why you come down here fe torment me spirit?"

Faced with the prospect of becoming dog meat, Jim began to back off unsteadily, sweating profusely. The gravity of the situation was clear: a trio of angry Johnsons were on the warpath and Jim didn't fancy arguing with their machetes. If ever there was a time when he wished Robert Johnson was around, it was now. But the one coolheaded Johnson was dead and his family held Jim responsible for his death. Marian made a sudden dash at him swinging the lethal sword in the air like a crazy person. Jim dodged Marian's lunge, the blade missing him by inches and as she wheeled it around again Jim dived to the ground to avoid what could have been a fatal blow.

Suddenly, the sound of bullets cracked into the sky and everyone froze. A police car had pulled up in the Johnsons' yard unnoticed and the driver, Detective Barnabas Collins, now stood watching them. "Dat's enough!" he commanded, walking slowly towards them, his arm relaxed at his side with his regulation revolver pointing innocently at the ground. "You lucky, y'know," the policeman said to Jim as he came closer. "Nex' time, lef' the explaining fe we fe do, y'hear?"

He helped Jim to his feet, all the while keeping a watchful eye on Marian who still seemed intent on performing an amputation on the man she blamed for her husband's grim and untimely demise.

Kai was now level with Marian and managed to take the machete from her, his firm hand restraining her from any further action. Her stare was bitter and Jim looked away.

"Yeah," Jim thanked the officer quietly, before picking himself up and walking away, all the time wondering who the policeman was and why he had never seen him around here before.

FIVE
Black Thursday

The parish of St Thomas had been in a deep state of shock since the tragic day when the two corpses had been found. The murderer had already been dubbed the Swinger, but their grief was tinged with something more sinister as wild rumours started to spread. "How had one man been able to string up another?" several people had asked. It was a question that was on everyone's lips. But then someone had started a rumour that the police believed the murders had been carried out by a duppy. The rumour spread like wildfire. And all because one of the corpses had been found with a birdfoot vaguely nearby. It was a similar trademark to that of a killer executed over thirty years ago.

The maniac, nicknamed Birdfoot, had killed sixteen times in a reign of terror lasting seven months. His victims were mostly women and their children, and once he'd killed he would push a severed bird's foot up their noses as evidence of his own twisted mind.

The possibility of such a recurrence of misfortune had really stoked the burning imaginations of the more adventurous reporters of the local and national press. One newspaper even linked the sinister practice of obeah to the killings, claiming that the dead must have been the unwitting victims of 'science'. It was these reports that spurred Detective Collins to pull out all the stops and gather together all the information he could on many of the unsolved cases of past years to see if there was a link.

The macabre cuttings on the killings did not unduly trouble a man who had investigated many murders and had survived two machete attacks and four shootings, but even this detective couldn't help feeling distaste at some of the crimes. One tale was reported particularly vividly and was known as the 'Hide and Seek' murder.

A family of four had been out all day at a church convention and had returned to find their home turned upside down as if burglars had gone on the rampage. After reporting the incident to the local police they settled down for a restful night. When they had all gone to bed the murderer, who had been hiding out in the backyard, sneaked back in and butchered the whole family bar a little girl who had managed to escape by hiding undetected underneath a couple of loose floorboards in a bedroom.

The unfortunate girl, the only witness to the horrific slaughter of her family, was never able to assist the police in their inquires as her mental state following the outrage would ensure that she spent the rest of her life in institutions for the insane.

Barnabas Collins was frantically trying to get more information on the 'Hide and Seek' murder and others from central records in Kingston. But the detective's efforts were hampered by slow communications and incompetent officers at the Kingston end. He was still hanging on on the telephone when they told him the only available car to send the information in was out of petrol, which would delay the arrival of the evidence another day.

Annoyed and frustrated by the sorry state of the communication channels in the Jamaican Police Force, Barnabas wiped the sweat from his brow and glanced briefly around the small police station. There had been many times in the last thirty years that he had wondered if this line of work was really for him, but he couldn't give up the power he felt it gave him. When he was interrogating a suspect he got a real rush from seeing the fright on their faces. It was the life he had chosen and the only life he could envisage. Despite the melodrama he had been successful investigating almost a hundred murders up and down the country. He was so good at solving mysteries that he had been called specially from Kingston to clear up the heinous double murders which had rocked the tiny parish of St Thomas.

Shuffling the newspaper cuttings around, Collins' eyes fell on something which caused him to straighten up in his chair and frown. It was a cutting from four or five years back. Two bodies had been found hanging from the same tree on consecutive mornings. It was in another parish on the other side of the island. Though the perpetrator of that crime was never caught, there had been no more hanging bodies and eventually the case was filed under 'Unsolved Murders'. At the time one of the inhabitants of the small village had reportedly said, "Dem did all wan' obeah for bad bad t'ings, so the obeah work back on dem." An interesting idea but not really feasible, thought the detective. Still, Barnabas decided to send for the relevant police file anyway.

Six
The Race

Was she dreaming? Or was this for real? Suddenly, her body spun around, as if of its own will and before she could figure out what was happening, she was floating out of the front door of her home and out of their front yard. She floated over the gap in the fence where the gate should have been, and for a moment hovered there above the dusty track outside. Then her body was spun around again and before she knew it, she was floating down the track, down to the big bend in the road. There she was floating above the heads of people she knew well and some who she knew less well. There was Mr Brown, her favourite teacher and there was Syd Johnson, her sworn enemy. And there, further down the track, was the White Woman and, over across the road, the dreaded Ole Miller house.

She suddenly felt afraid and didn't want to be floating anymore. No, she didn't want to go in there. No, she definitely didn't want to go in there. Suddenly, the gate of Ole Miller's house creaked open, as if by itself, leaving a gap wide enough to pass through. It stood like that, invitingly.

Against her will, Ella started floating towards it. "No!" she heard herself screaming but nobody else seemed to hear. "No! Nooo! Nooooo!" But she continued floating, now through the gate and above the overgrown front yard. Then, almost as if she was expected, the long boarded-up front-door swung open as she approached the house.

"Ella!" she heard a voice call as she floated into the darkened interior of the Miller house for the first time. Her heart pounded hard. She turned her head in the direction of the voice and to her relief, she saw her brother Bill, at the front-door behind her. He had come to help her after all.

"Me see somet'ing move upstairs, El," Bill said in hushed tones.

"Is lie you ah tell, you jus' waan frighten me."

"Me nah lie," Bill hissed. "Me see wha' me see."

That was all Ella needed to hear, she wanted to float out of there, but her brother was determined. He had begun to mount the stairs slowly, softly, silently. Ella floated after him.

"Nuh bother go up deh, Bill," Ella begged in a loud whisper. But her warning failed to deter her brother who continued as carefully as he could up the creaky and dusty staircase. Ella floated after him.

"Yuh senses mussa leave you," she squealed. "Come back." She didn't want to go up those steps and into the darkness above but at the same time she couldn't leave her brother.

"Me nah go nowhere," Bill replied. He was determined to discover the mystery of Ole Miller. "Dis time, me ah go do it."

He made his way up, treading on each step with caution. Just as he got to the landing, with Ella floating reluctantly behind him, a voice boomed from the darkness: "AH WHO DAT INNA ME HOUSE?!"

The cry took Bill by surprise and he lost his balance falling over backwards all the way down the bottom of the stairs.

"IF AH PICKNEY, ME AH GO NYAM UNUH FE DINNER!!" the voice laughed.

Neither Bill nor Ella needed to hear any more. Bill picked himself up and fled out the front-door after his sister who had already floated out and was heading for the safety of her bed without turning to glance back at Ole Miller's house.

Suddenly the pictures went blank and darkness was her only company. It was strange. She seemed to be wide awake yet she was unable to get up. On waking up, Ella found her head felt heavy, throbbing as if a big bell had been struck inside it. After her wash, the queasy feeling lightened up somewhat and the big event of the day made her forget the headache still lingering. No-one or nothing was going to stop her from running the big race and winning it. She was so excited that she would have even skipped breakfast if it wasn't for her mother. Mom Butler forced her to sit and eat some callaloo and fried plantain.

"Yuh cyan run on empty stomach. An' wha'ppen to yuh; how your eyes look tired so? Yuh feel a'right?"

Ella dismissed her mother's concern.

"Me a'right, Mom..."

A big sign publicising the race was draped above the entrance to the school. Freshly cut flowers had been arranged around the grounds and a huge table had been placed to the right of the main building. "Dat mussi where the cup an' the medals dem ah hand out," said Ella, heading towards the registration desk at the front of the school.

Mr Brown was in charge of registration and seemed to be enjoying the day for which he had dressed up specially in the same suit he had worn to his wedding. His teeth sparkled in the morning sunlight and his hair was shiny and immaculate.

"Who you ah dress up for?" Ella asked innocently.

"You did seh somet'ing?" Mr Brown queried, with a hint of embarrassment. "So you ah go tek on the big bwoy dem?"

Ella nodded slowly, a sudden feeling of dizziness overcoming her. She hadn't eaten much of the plantain and callaloo at breakfast that morning, so maybe she needed something to supplement it. She had some mangoes in her school bag and as soon as she had registered she would have to eat a couple.

"Feel you have a chance then?" Mr Brown continued, smiling.

"Of course," Ella nodded, before going in search of a quiet corner of the school grounds to sit down for a moment. She found a spot near the washroom where she could collect her thoughts. She hoped she wasn't becoming ill. She took out a mango and bit into it, pulling the skin free and sucking out the orange flesh.. Then she looked up to see her brother as he stood chatting to a trio of girls. When Bill noticed his sister over by herself he told the girls he would 'check' them later and came over.

"So wha'ppen, El?"

"Not'n, " Ella replied softly. She nodded towards the girls. "You have some new friends then?"

Bill looked back swiftly and smiled at the girls. "Naa," he said uncomfortably, "me jus' ah mek idle chat."

"You know wha' old time people seh: Idle dawg teef…"

Ella's laughter was cut short by the appearance of Skully

McLean, already dressed in his shorts and singlet, ready for the race.

"Me hear seh you ah go beat me inna the race," Skully grinned.

"You shouldn't believe everyt'ing y'hear, Skully, because one day it may come true," Ella retorted.

Skully burst out laughing. "So you really feel you can win then?"

"Bwoy, me jus' ah go run an' see how it go…"

At that point Bill intervened, "Rivals shouldn't chat before the fight, y'know," he said jokingly.

"We nah fight, we jus' ah run," Skully replied.

Organisation for the sports day was as good as could be expected for the limited money available to the school for such events. Some of the pupils' parents were in attendance, though for most students they were to run without the support of their friends and family who were either too busy working hard or lived too far away from the school to be there. Only a few minor problems threatened to mar the occasion—namely 'Footsore' Sinclair and 'Shady' Brown's disagreement, which quickly broke out into a fight, over who won the one hundred yards sprint, one of the earlier races. A furious Mr Brown settled the argument by banishing both boys from the rest of the sports day and awarding the race to third placed Ivadeen Seymour, whose joy at winning something for the first time in her life brought many a cheer from those supporters of the underdog.

Ella had watched with interest as all the other races took place but, like everybody else, was waiting for the main event—the Big Race.

Eventually, it was time.

"Today has been a wonderful success," Mr Brown announced proudly to everybody present. "Yes, a wonderful success," he repeated, trying hard to mask his natural Jamaican tongue. "But it has not finished yet, because now it's time for the Big Race. So all dem children who waan tek part, come forward."

No sooner had he finished speaking than there was a mad rush towards him. Skully McLean bobbed his head up and down confidently as he eyed the competition talking amongst themselves. He wasn't alone at the front, however. Junior Tucker was there. Junior had beaten Skully before on a number of occasions, but was still considered second best. Today he had something to prove. Miriam Davies was also there, she was the best girl runner in her year and was very confident about doing well. Ella was with them.

In total sixteen runners showed themselves; and Mr Brown decided that that was enough. "What a wonderful response," he said, grinning from ear to ear. He made sure all the children were attentive before going over the route step by step, taking care to go through every little detail.

"Well, me sure everybody know the route..."

Ella swapped a final glance with Miriam Davies before looking into the crowd for Bill. She spotted him and waved quickly then turned her mind on the job at hand. Then Mr Brown called the runners into line in preparation for the start.

At the starting line, Ella began to feel nervous. She looked down at her feet. Like everybody else she was running barefoot and she was counting on her little feet to see her through to victory.

Suddenly, she started feeling dizzy again and before she knew it her head started spinning and her eyes blurring...

"Unuh ready?" she heard the distant voice of Mr Brown. Ella sucked in as much air as her lungs would allow and slowly breathed it out again. She gazed upwards, at the shimmering heat patterns from the sun's dazzling rays. It was too late to say that she wasn't ready.

"Go!" Mr Brown cried out, starting the race.

Dirt and dust went flying as all sixteen children kicked into motion and propelled themselves towards the school gate through which they squeezed en masse. Angus Wilson showed first, bursting through the crowd and sprinting to the front. That was bravado on his part and everyone knew he wouldn't last the distance. The following group was led by Skully McLean, with Junior Tucker, 'Ole Foot' Simpson and Miriam Davies in close contention. Ella was off the pace, but she was in touch and moving easily. The rest of the pack were already beginning to tail off, such was the pace Angus was setting, running like 'duppy ah chase him'.

They were running through some of the most spectacular scenery anywhere in Jamaica, up hill and down valley, along the many twists and turns of the road. Until thirty years or so ago, the road was part of a network of mule trails kept open by foresters and farmers who used it to transport their produce to market. But with the changing economic patterns farmers no longer depended on mules but began to transport their produce to market by truck. This particular trail was not allowed to fall into disrepair and be overgrown like others, however; it was to become the main road in the area. One year, a network of bulldozers arrived to cut a dirt road, replacing and expanding the old trail.

All the children had been warned to stay on the road and avoid taking any shortcuts. With the mystery of the recent deaths still unexplained, nobody was prepared to take that chance anyway.

Sweat began to pour from Ella's face as she felt the pace of the race pick up again, streams of sweat. Somehow, she kept going, running like in a dream, trying to clear her head. She was breathing heavily. Amongst the crowd who speckled the route, she could hear both shouts of encouragement as well as one or two cries of abuse—Syd Johnson's amongst them. All through this, Ella fought to keep her mind on the business at hand. Tony Morrison and Sandra Barratt pulled up alongside her, working hard to get back into the race. Ella hadn't imagined that the pace would be this intense and was trying her best not to burn herself out.

"You a'right?" Tony Morrison panted, the struggle to survive the momentum telling in his voice.

Ella nodded and, gulping for air, smiled confidently. "You nuh a'right?" Tony continued. "You ah struggle. You bettah start run before you mek dem deh tactic beat you."

Ella's feet and legs relaxed a little as she adjusted to the faster than usual pace. Her arms were flowing now, not pumping like before. She had full concentration and for the first time she felt in control.

"Wha' you mean tactic?" she asked, breathing hard.

"Dem deh bwoy ah front seh...dem ah go murder you with dem quick start...an' by the time you ketch a mile you nuh have no use to nobody nah yuhself," Tony advised.

"So a plan?" Ella cried out. "Dem nah beat me with no plan yah," she summed up, extending her stride. She looked ahead and could see the others in front. It was early days yet.

The route wound towards the Cane and Tobacco Farm. Angus Wilson, as predicted, had fallen off the leading group and was going backwards as fast as he had sprung to the front. Miriam Davies breezed into the lead. The pace had eased and the leaders had settled into a methodical rhythm with all contenders looking strong. Tony Morrison and Sandra Barratt had worked hard behind the leading group and pulled Ella along with them. Skully McLean and Junior Tucker seemed to be testing each other, running their own private contest. 'Ole Foot' Simpson had fallen foul of a large stone in the road which ended his race prematurely. Ella soon left Tony and Sandra behind and was now just behind the leaders. The pace was beginning to hot up again. There was just one mile to go.

Ella's confidence grew with every step. She had moved onto the shoulder of Junior Tucker who was vying for space on the inside bend of the road. Skully shut the space down, however, and Junior was forced to ease back and track him. Miriam Davies was now beginning to falter. Her legs could no longer maintain the driving pace which had sustained her in front position; they suddenly gave way. She threw her arms up in resignation. For her, it was all over.

Ella glanced back briefly to see Miriam cussing and throwing her arms around wildly, she was very upset. It was now a three-horse race.

Ella felt her heart tighten and her breathing become shorter. She wasn't feeling the pace, but she was still feeling unwell. She tried to yawn and take a deep breath to stoke up her second wind. It wouldn't come. She pressed on regardless.

Skully McLean attempted to take control by increasing the pace. Ella's feet matched the sudden burst of speed, so did Junior Tucker's.

Skully's face said it all. His devastating kick had been ineffective and signs of strain began to appear in that previously invincible armour. Then, simultaneously, all three runners suddenly saw the school buildings looming in the distance, with nearly the entire school outside, cheering them on.

Junior Tucker suddenly broke free to make his bid. It was ill-timed, however. It urged Skully even more and he caught up with his main rival, even overtaking Junior. Ella's feet seemed to have wings and she eased past him also and remained at Skully's shoulder, determination etched on her face. There were only two horses in it now.

Seeing that the little girl was still at his heels, Skully's face contorted and his shoulders tightened to give it everything he had. To lose to Junior was one thing, but to allow Ella to come anywhere near his victory would still be embarrassing. He pumped his arms powerfully in a gallant parade to victory. Ella seemed resigned to second place, but she had one last effort in her. Skully McLean was only a few strides away. Ella grimaced and dug deep and felt the power surge through her legs. All she could hear were the cheers of encouragement from her fellow pupils as she eased up on Skully's inside. Something remarkable was about to happen, and the spectators could sense it as they saw Skully's confidence drain from his face.

There were about two hundred yards remaining. It was going to go to the wire. Ella threw herself into top gear and, with only inches to go, managed to pip Skully to the post.

Almost immediately, a deafening roar of approval sang out from the spectators as they rushed the winner. Ella was exhausted, but managed to throw her arms in the air in a victory salute before collapsing in a heap on the dusty school grounds.

"You do it, El, you do it!" Bill screamed as he rushed over to his sister and picked her up. Her body was limp, lifeless. All her energy had been sucked through those wiry legs and now that she had finished the race she felt an acute pain in her stomach. She managed to remain standing with Bill's help, her breath returning slowly. She noticed the disconsolate figure of Skully McLean who was weeping uncontrollably.

"Bad luck," she said genuinely, stretching out her hand, sportsmanlike.

"Yeah," he replied, trying hard to mask his tears. "Wicked run, Ella, today ah yuh day. But me still the best," Skully teased.

Only four runners didn't finish the race and they each had good reason: 'Ole Foot' Simpson had cracked his big toe; Devon James and Robert Hanson had had a disagreement and ended up in a brawl en-route and Ivan Smith was waylaid by some friends who had convinced him to play truant with them.

Even as all her friends were congratulating her, Ella noticed a long face amongst them. It was a timid-looking Jacqueline Evans. Everyone was surprised to see her as this term she had truanted more than she had attended class.

"Whe' Bubsy deh?" Ruth asked, referring to Jacqueline's 'boyfriend', from whom she was inseparable.

Jacqueline shrugged her shoulders.

"Wha' wrong with you?" Ella asked, noticing tears welling up in her classmate's eyes.

"Not'n wrong," Jacqueline replied, sniffing hard.

"Somet'ing must wrong if you nuh with Bubsy."

Jacqueline didn't respond immediately. When she finally replied there was a look of anguish and puzzlement on her face.

"Bubsy jus' run off an' lef' me down ah the Cane an' Tobacco Farm. Me nuh know where the bwoy turn, him jus' gone."

As everybody in the school knew, she and Bubsy did

90

everything together, including truancy. With no sign of him, she had decided to return to school in the hope that he would show up before the day was over.

"Nuh min' yaar," Ella said. "Y'know how Bubsy stay, duppy mussa chase him."

Jacqueline managed a smile and a nod.

Just then Mr Brown appeared among the crowd which had gathered around the victorious Ella.

"Me see you mek it," he said, staring pointedly at Jacqueline.

"Sorry me did late, Sah; me lickle sister did tek sick an' me haffe look after her 'til me mudda come from market," Jacqueline whined apologetically.

"Hhmm," Mr Brown grunted as he accepted the weak excuse. "Later you can explain all the other days me nevah see you ah school."

Mr Brown noticed the tears in Jacqueline's eyes also and asked her what the matter was. Jacqueline explained again that while she was 'on my way to school', she had met Bubsy who was also 'on his way to school' and that her last sight of him had been at the Cane & Tobacco Farm.

In light of the recent murders, the police should be notified if Bubsy didn't show up soon, Mr Brown decided. He was reluctant to call them immediately because, like everybody else, he knew of Bubsy's relationship with Jacqueline and their games and their reluctance to attend school. He comforted Jacqueline and told her that they would wait a few minutes for Bubsy. If he was 'on his way to school', he would no doubt show up soon. Meanwhile, the day was almost over and all that remained was the awards ceremony.

"This day has been a great success," Mr Brown announced to the whole school, once they had quietened down. He

91

plucked a small trophy from the registration table in front of him and held it high. "This trophy I present to Ella Louise Butler, for her victory in the Big Race. Dis win was truly magnificent and me sure unuh will agree was a race to remember."

Ella stepped up to claim her prize, holding it up high. As the rapturous applause died down, Ella held her hand up to silence the crowd, as if she were some celebrity.

"Bwoy," she began, "me nuh have not'n much fe seh, but thank you to all the teacher dem fe putting on the race, an' fe the people who did run inna it. Me know me did win the race, but respect to Skully, Junior and Miriam, 'cause dem bad."

The crowd erupted into cheers again. Ella smiled and then suddenly felt an intense dizziness which caused her to sway slightly on her feet. She felt weak.

They had to call a taxi to get Ella home that afternoon, she was too weak to make the journey otherwise, even with the help of her brother.

Mom Butler sensed there was something wrong the moment she saw the taxi pull up outside her house, with her son and daughter in the back seat. She rushed out quickly and cried to the Lord to have 'mercy' on her child before helping Bill to get his sister inside.

"Ella, what happen? Yuh a'right?"

The question was unnecessary for it was quite clear that Ella was not herself. Ella didn't answer her mother either. Apparently oblivious to everything around her, she simply stared vacantly ahead.

"Wha'ppen to you, is dream you ah dream?" Mom repeated. Then she gasped.

"Ella! Ella, talk to me! Oh my God…"

Mom Butler couldn't understand it. All the signs said that her daughter had a fever, her temperature was high and sweat poured down her face, yet Ella's forehead and face felt ice cold to the touch. And she seemed to be in some kind of trance, from which she was unable to snap out of. Mom Butler looked down at her daughter with fright in her eyes. She had never seen her like this before. She didn't know what to do and all that came to mind was to lift her, gently, and lay her down on her bed, which she did, all the time stroking her tenderly while talking to her, hoping for a sign, a movement. Smelling salts and a face rub with some strong pimento rum failed to bring any improvement to Ella's condition. After almost an hour, her eyes closed and Mom Butler cried out loud, fearing the worst.

Bill felt a chill go through his body. He was scared. Mom Butler chartered a taxi and told her son to go with it and bring back Dr Gardener, the nearest physician. After another hour, the doctor arrived. He was an elderly man who had practiced in the area for nearly fifty years but he had been trained to deal with the most common ailments and while he was adept at prescribing treatments for worms or constipation, anything he was unable to understand was usually put down to the local 'science'. After about ten minutes with his patient, Dr Gardener concluded that there was nothing he could do to alter Ella's condition in any way. Eventually, after promising he'd be back in the morning, he departed.

It wasn't until early evening that Mom Butler decided to send an urgent message through Bill to her husband down at the Cane & Tobacco Farm.

By the time Jim got home from work his daughter was sprawled out on the bed, half on, half off.

"Ella!" Jim cried, forgetting his own fatigue and rushing to her bedside. Ella still did not respond.

"Ella!" Jim cried out again, holding her arm which hung limply off the bed. She was sweating profusely, writhing and moaning to herself deliriously. Bill looked confused and stood silently watching. He'd never seen his sister like this and it scared him.

"What happen?" Jim bellowed as he felt Ella's forehead. Despite the sweat, she was cold to his touch.

Bill simply looked at his father with terror in his eyes. He had no answer. What could he say? One moment she was okay and running in a race, the next moment she had collapsed.

Mom Butler came bustling into the room then, holding a basin in one hand and a cup in the other.

"Move!" she ordered, putting the basin and cup on the floor and pushing Bill out of the way. She knelt down, soaked a cloth out in the water and applied it to Ella's forehead. Once she'd repeated this a few times, Ella seemed to settle. Mom waited until her daughter was completely at rest before getting up from the floor. Bill registered the look on his mother's face, a look he had never seen before. Fear.

"Me baby sick," she told her husband in a shaky voice. "She sick bad an' the doctor can't help her."

"The doctor come already?" Jim asked, wringing his hands anxiously.

Mom Butler nodded, "Yes, the doctor come an' gone. Him seh dat him nuh understand wha'ppen to her, but she sick bad."

"How y'mean, Mom?" Jim asked, thoughts running through his mind like crazy. Right now he could only think of the worst. Everything seemed unreal, like a bad dream he was having. He had already been through this kind of fear before. He remembered. This was how he'd felt when Little Jakie had died in his truck.

Mom looked at Ella and flinched as if a cold shudder had passed through her body. "Science... obeah business!" she cried loudly and started to cry. The suppressed emotion of the whole afternoon flooded out as Bill went to his mother and hugged her closely.

Jim Butler stood motionless, staring at his daughter. He was beginning to deal with the reality and as he did so, began to work out the options in his head. This was a route he hoped he would never have to take. If Mom Butler was right, and there was just a slight chance that she might be, there was only one thing to do...

Mom Butler regained her composure and told Bill to wait outside. Bill wanted to protest, but the tone of his mother's voice told him it was better to comply. He went and sat in the backyard reluctantly.

"Wha' we can do, Mom? We can't jus' sit an' watch..." Jim turned to his wife. He was beginning to feel the strain and looked tired and worried. Mom Butler nodded. She had been considering the options also. As far as she was concerned, there was only one thing to do.

Finally, Jim Butler made the decision. He sent Bill to summon PickneyDaddy.

SEVEN
Obeah Business

The sun set gloriously, lighting the hilltop like a giant orange beam of light. All through the taxi ride, and even now as they were climbing the steep hill leading to the isolated set of buildings, PickneyDaddy had not uttered a word. Bill was breathing heavily, sweat running down his neck and trickling down his back. He hadn't wanted to go, but his father just didn't want to leave Ella's side. She'd always been his favourite.

Bill took a quick glance down at the smattering of roofs below, at the village he knew only by name, a place exclusively for those who resided there or had direct 'business' there. He was glad that they were not going to Stylehut, but to the hilltop compound overlooking it and that they were not going to visit an obeah man, but a healer.

The name Stylehut wasn't on any map and was hardly mentioned or referred to and even then only big people spoke of it. But Bill had apparently come of age through the ordeal that his family was now going through. In his heart he was

96

scared, fearing he was about to lose his only sister—his friend and partner for all those years since losing his younger brother. Yet Bill had quickly submerged that feeling in a steely determination to be a man and face up to the responsibilities thrown upon him. He concluded that his father knew best and seemed to have sobered up from his usual drunken state. Now, he himself, Bill, had started to understand the forces at play in the present drama. At fourteen, he had heard enough hard information and half-facts about the dangerous practices of the obeah worker to have formed his own opinion about its role in his sister's sudden illness.

Climbing behind the brooding old man, fretting with his whole body for Ella's life, Bill knew he was about to be witness to things only an adult should. After today, he was to be a man. The white and blue flags of the compound were getting close now, bathed in the golden rays of the sun. For the first time PickneyDaddy stopped and waited for the youth to catch up with him. When he turned, the old man seemed neither out of breath nor affected by the long climb in any way. His face bore an almost sad expression Bill had never seen before.

"Yuh can't repeat anyt'ing you gwan hear, to nobody…yuh understand?"

Bill nodded. PickneyDaddy turned and approached the wooden gates, then stopped at the entrance. Bill stood by his side and watched as a tall, thin-faced woman with a white turban beckoned them to enter as she opened the gates up. Once inside, the first thing Bill noticed was the square concrete floor with tall poles in each corner supporting the flags.

"Good night. I come to see the Shepherd."

Bill felt the eyes of the woman stop on him briefly, then she nodded courteously. They followed her to a small house on the right, near a large concrete reservoir with sloping edges. Bill

97

saw several women, dressed similarly to their guide, engaged in what sounded to him like a church service under a thatched-roof open area in the centre of the yard. The long shadows of evening had started to descend, adding to his apprehension. He saw PickneyDaddy say something to the woman as they stopped by the open door of a room, then she climbed the two steps and entered. The chanting voices from the service were drifting in the evening air, over the steady rhythm of the crickets' song. Then the woman reappeared and showed them in. She left after having them sit on wooden chairs. Soon after, a short, brown man, dressed in a white shirt and blue cotton pants, walked in from inside the house. His deeply creased features lit up as he saw PickneyDaddy.

"Praise the Lord, Bredda Simon, welcome."

"Praise the Lord." PickneyDaddy repeated.

Bill saw him get up so he did too, showing manners. The two men shook hands, then the Shepherd sat across from them. He had acknowledged Bill's salutation with a nod, seeming interested only in PickneyDaddy. The two old men were friends from way back, having lived all their life in the same neighbourhood and spent many of their youthful years doing what young men do. But Shepherd Bennett, as church members and patients called him, had responded to an early calling, which had run in his family for several generations, to become the leader of a revival church.

The Shepherd's healing work had people with various types of illnesses visiting him from miles around. With prayers and rituals, he had delivered hundreds from the spells and pains inflicted on some of his fellow countrymen by the greed, vengeance or envy of others. That the centre had thrived for so long in the midst of, or above, as it were, a village like Stylehut, was testimony enough to its power against the dark forces thriving in the neighbourhood.

"Bredda Bennett, me ah come fe some help..."

Soon, PickneyDaddy and the healer were engaged in a quiet conversation, which seemed to become quieter with every word until Bill could hear nothing of what was being said. The conversation was not for Bill's ears and PickneyDaddy would make sure that he remained ignorant of the healer's revelations. Thus the earlier advice that Bill should tell no-one about what he heard here seemed irrelevant.

Later, he would tell Jim what Shepherd Bennett had to say. He would tell Jim that the healer had 'seen' the person who went to an obeah worker in the first place was now dead. Before they departed, the Shepherd handed PickneyDaddy a bottle filled with a liquid to wash Ella's face, hands and feet and told his friend that he must bring Ella to the Centre early in the morning.

The next morning, PickneyDaddy, Jim Butler and Bill carried the unconscious Ella up the hill in a donkey cart. Her condition seemed to have worsened overnight and had kept Jim up at her bedside throughout. Shepherd Bennett was awaiting them when they arrived. The first thing he did was ask a few of the women in the Centre to bathe the child in a hot herbal bath. Meanwhile, he prepared the chapel for the ceremony which was about to take place. It was more than thirty minutes before the women returned carrying Ella wrapped in a blanket.

With her father's help, Shepherd Bennett carried her into the chapel, followed by the others, and placed the child on the dusty floor inside. Then, he proceeded to anoint Ella, while the women formed a circle around him and began to chant, performing a sort of dance in a counterclockwise motion. PickneyDaddy whispered to Jim that this was called 'travelling', then the two stood silently watching as the women danced themselves into a trance, bending forwards and backwards from head to waist and chopping the air with both hands, while chanting in a soft hiss as they inhaled deeply then a loud grunt as they exhaled.

The ceremony went on for several hours. Bill, PickneyDaddy and Jim watched silently as one by one the women fell into a trance. Now, there was only one woman left standing. The others lay in a heaving heap on the ground. This last woman stood tensely for a moment, ready to 'war' with the spirit possessing Ella, which she alone had been chosen to defeat. Her chanting grew noisier, her dancing speeded up, becoming louder and louder and faster and faster as she wrestled with an unseen enemy. Eventually, her chant became a piercing scream in the tiny chapel and she spun like a tornado in a tight circle around the sick child, forcing the evil spirit to leave her body. Finally, with a deafening cry, the woman crumbled in an exhausted heap on the ground.

Jim flashed a look at the healer, wondering what to do next. He was about to go to his child, when Shepherd Bennett raised his hand for him to be patient a moment longer.

They all watched in silence as slowly, very slowly, there was a twitch of Ella's leg. Then her fingers started moving, feeling the dirt beneath them. Ella's eyes opened, one at a time, as she regained consciousness. Bill looked over at his father with a big smile on his face. This was the first time in almost twenty-four hours that Ella had shown any sign of improvement. Jim's watery eyes told the story of how he felt. But it wasn't over yet, Ella was to be bathed once again before it was time to go home.

Ella was still far from normal. Shepherd Bennett informed Jim that his daughter now needed to rest as much as possible. As they carried her onto the donkey cart ready to ferry her homewards, the healer turned to Jim with some more news.

"One t'ing me did forget fe seh…you will know who me ah talk, so me nah mention no names…you see dis same obeah work wha' mek yuh daughter sick, ah the same obeah wha' tek 'way yuh lickle bwoy when yuh deh inna the rum shop."

Jim almost collapsed from the healer's words. Was Shepherd Bennett sure? The healer reminded Jim that he had been gifted with the power of 'seeing' and that he was never wrong.

"You must know yuh enemies…" he warned, handing Jim two extra bottles of liquid to bath himself and his family in daily.

Jim Butler weighed everything in his mind on the journey home, the words of the healer echoing in his mind. He was trying to interpret the Shepherd's vision. If what he was thinking was correct, he knew who his 'enemies' were and their family would pay dearly. But he needed to be sure, he needed a little more evidence. The Shepherd had said that the person responsible for putting obeah on Ella was now dead. No matter, his family would have to pay for the sins of the father, Jim decided, and for the death of Little Jakie also.

As far as Jim was concerned, if the Shepherd was right about the one, he was right about the other, that much was obvious. This was what he wanted to believe to relieve himself of the burden of responsibility for his youngest son's death. And the Johnsons had a long history of obeah in their family. All he needed was some evidence that it was them and he would get them off his land. "Know yuh enemies" the Shepherd had said. Well, Jim thought to himself, he had a plan that would expose his enemies.

Mom Butler had sat by Ella's bedside all evening, unconvinced that the visit to Shepherd Bennett was a success. Even though her husband, confident of Ella's gradual recovery, had decided to leave the house, saying he had 'business' to attend to that evening, as far as she could see, her daughter was still sick.

She fixed her gaze on Ella. Her daughter was slumped in a deep sleep, with a troubled expression on her face.

Mom Butler sat helplessly, unsure of what to do. Seeing her daughter in the state she was now in had terrified her emotions into action. Jim was the man she loved; the only man she had ever loved and all the petty arguments of the last few months now seemed unimportant. As for Ella, she couldn't even comprehend losing another child. With fat tears rolling down her cheeks, Mom Butler leaned over and planted a tender kiss on her daughter's cheek. Ella's unconscious moan lifted Mom Butler's spirits momentarily, but her daughter had been moaning like that for some time now. She squeezed Ella's hand tightly before releasing her grip.

When Bill entered the bedroom, his mother was sobbing softly to herself while mumbling something incomprehensible. She spun her head around as soon as her son came in.

The first thing Bill noticed was Ella slumped in the bed, still unconscious, but with sweat pouring down her brow.

"She jus' get worse an' worse," Mom Butler said, motioning to her daughter. "She under the obeah...me haffe stop dis before you all get affect."

Bill nodded. Ella looked really ill. "She ah go a'right," he told his mother reassuringly.

"It mussi obeah," Mom Butler continued, absentmindedly fixing the scarf on her head. She threw up her hands in despair. Bill went over to his mother and placed a comforting hand around her shoulders. Mom Butler just continued shaking her head. There were things that Bill didn't understand, how could he? He was just a child, after all. How could he really understand what obeah meant?

After a moment's silence, Mom Butler said, "me ah go send you down ah Massa Allen yard fe go find out somet'ing fe me."

"A'right, me know where him live," Bill replied.

"Yes, me know, but me ah go send you with PickneyDaddy, because from desso unuh going haffe go ah Honey Hole down ah Stylehut fe go buy somet'ing fe yuh sister..."

"Honey Hole!" Blood seeped away from Bill's face. "Dat deh place deh full ah duppy an' t'ing..."

"Me a'ready aarks PickneyDaddy and him agree to go with you, Bill. You will help yuh sister more if you go."

Bill was reluctant to do as his mother asked, this was one trip he wasn't looking forward to making, he would rather wait until his father came home. Mom Butler reminded him that his father had gone to the rum shop and she didn't know if he would be back this week let alone this night. Meanwhile, what would they do if Ella took a turn for the worse? They had to have some more help for her, just in case.

At that moment, PickneyDaddy came in and asked whether Bill was ready to go. He had gone home to pick up his machete.

"Nuh min' yaar," PickneyDaddy told Mom Butler comfortingly.

"She ah go a'right," Bill said, coming out of the bedroom. He was as concerned for his sister as everyone else. All he wanted was for things to go back to how they used to be. But he wasn't sure about this obeah business. Bill started to sweat but it seemed like he had no choice.

"Hurry back!" Mom called after them as Bill followed PickneyDaddy out. "Yuh sister need the medicine quick time."

Massa Allen gazed into PickneyDaddy's eyes as if searching for something, a sign perhaps, then he pulled out a small box from under a cabinet. He fumbled with the string around the box for a moment before it gave way. He reached inside the box and clenched something in his hand, passing it to PickneyDaddy in a surreptitious exchange.

Bill watched the proceedings with some bemusement. He guessed what was going on, but at the moment he was more concerned with the fact that as soon as they had finished here they would have to go to Stylehut, where the darkest secrets of the universe were regularly practiced, and he wasn't looking forward to that.

"O...o...one t...t...t'ing me must tell you," Massa Allen stammered.

"Is wha'?" PickneyDaddy asked.

"W...w...w...w...whe' y...y...you ah g..g...g...go, 'n...n...nuff obeah man d...d...d...deh deh. S...s...some ah d...d...dem w...w...wicked to raas but dem s...s...seem nice but w...will work b...b...b...bad science on unuh fe not'n at all. Obeah man daughter always p...p...pretty. But beautiful woman, b...beautiful trouble. M...m...m...m...mek s...s...s...sure y...you nuh l...l...look 'pon dem too l...l...long."

"Yes, me know," PickneyDaddy acknowledged.

"An' n...n...nuh...b...b...bother l...l...lose me somet'ing y...y...y'know," he reminded PickneyDaddy as an afterthought.

"Yuh business safe," PickneyDaddy responded, placing the flat, smooth stone Massa Allen had slipped him into the crocus bag that was slung over his shoulder. They waved as they left Massa Allen's house and inched past the guard dog.

Massa Allen called them back briefly, to hand PickneyDaddy something else.

"Tek d...d...dis...b...b...box, but nuh open it u...u...u...unless the obeah man get m....m...m...mad with you!" Massa Allen called after them before turning to beat his dog into obedience.

"See a taxi deh," PickneyDaddy said as he flagged it down. The taxi screeched to a halt just beyond them and moments later they crammed into the already over-crowded car.

"Move yuh leg nuh woman," PickneyDaddy screeched when a rather large lady unwittingly twisted her heel into his ankle as they climbed in.

"You ah eediat!" the woman blasted. "You see dat the dyam car ram so 'til it can't ram no more, an' me can't even move fe breed."

"Breed? Who ah talk 'bout breed," PickneyDaddy sniggered. "You too ole fe have pickney."

The woman looked perplexed at first, but it didn't take long for his comment to sink in.

"The dyam facety man!" she screamed. "Ah who you ah talk to so?"

"Sorry," PickneyDaddy apologized, smiling. But the woman simply kissed her teeth and without warning sent a stinging slap across PickneyDaddy's face. By the time she had followed through, PickneyDaddy's face had been turned the other way, such was its impact. Bill was fortunate enough to be sitting in the front seat of the car as he watched the smile drain away from PickneyDaddy's face. PickneyDaddy looked back in shock. "Cork yuh ears yaar pickney," he told his young charge before proceeding to cuss the woman until she had to call "one stop driver!" and step out of the car.

The sting of the slap persisted long after the taxi had continued on its journey and PickneyDaddy sat rubbing his cheek the rest of the way. "Jus' mek sure me nuh hear unuh chat dem deh word, 'cause me nuh waan unuh mammy come tell me not'n 'bout me ah teach unuh fe swear."

Bill nodded. Now that the incident was over he was able to have a little chuckle to himself at PickneyDaddy's expense.

By the time the taxi reached Honey Hole, Bill and PickneyDaddy were the only remaining passengers. Few ordinary citizens ventured this far unless they had some form of business there, business which they always kept close to their chests. Even the taxi drivers were loathe to drive this far and if PickneyDaddy hadn't agreed on paying an extra tariff, they would have had to walk the last stretch of their journey. Bill had never come this far before either and the village they now found themselves in seemed deserted.

The taxi had dropped them outside Duppy Bridge. Taxis from their area never ventured past Duppy Bridge. It was the unofficial border. Taxis ran from Sea Wharf and beyond, which was a short walk away.

Nothing grew in Duppy Bridge. It's soil was an unnatural

red—some said from the blood of those unfortunate souls who were foolish enough to linger in the area longer than was absolutely necessary. In reality, the soil of Duppy Bridge was soaked in the colour of fifty years of bauxite deposits from the aluminium factory up river, and looked like a desert in a jungle of lush vegetation.

Duppy Bridge was not so much a bridge, but a narrow stretch of land that bridged a gully. In the olden days it was said that ghosts lay in wait there to rob passers-by of their possessions.

"Ah lie!" said one disbelieving man, who promptly went to the bridge one night to prove that it was all nonsense and that the "duppy dem would ah 'fraid ah *me* before dem can come frighten me." He was never seen again. Some disbelievers still contended it was all a myth and that the missing man had disappeared to get away from his wife and gone to Kingston to live with his sweetheart; they even offered to provide his address, at a price, to anyone desperate enough to find out the truth. However, this didn't detract from the reality, that Duppy Bridge, because of its reputation, was a place most people feared.

Bill watched the taxi disappear until he noticed PickneyDaddy had trudged off.

"Is dis way," said PickneyDaddy and Bill hurried after him, unwilling to lose his friend and guide on this particular journey. They cut right across the barren stretch of Duppy Bridge and were soon in the thick of the bush that surrounded Stylehut.

"Me did see you ah look 'pon dat pretty girl inna the taxi back so," PickneyDaddy said with a wink of his eye.

107

Bill looked away with embarrassment, realizing his secret was out. His eyes were darting from side to side, trying to take in as much as he could of this mysterious place which he had heard about only in hushed tones and where, by all accounts, every other household practiced obeah.

"Who me?" he replied, playing fool to catch wise.

"Cho', who you ah fool? You know..."

Yes, Bill knew exactly. He was becoming a man in all the little ways that boys become men, and as such was engaged in those 'manly' pursuits which men have been engaged in for centuries before him. How could he be sitting in a car with a beautiful girl and not notice her? PickneyDaddy had obviously noticed her also, even though she was too young for him.

"One day..." PickneyDaddy promised, "one day me ah go tell you all 'bout woman...me ah go tell you everyt'ing... y'understand?"

Bill nodded shyly, a big grin on his face.

"For the moment, keep your mind on whe' we deh, 'cause dis ah one bad place. You can't trust anybody. 'Member what Massa Allen seh—you see 'nuff pretty gal yah, but dem is duppy fe true."

"Nuh bother with dat, PickneyDaddy," Bill started, "me nuh waan hear not'n 'bout duppy."

"No, man. Me nah chat to you 'bout dem sint'ing, but you see dat gal you did see inna the taxi, you must be careful. Ah jus' dat me ah talk 'bout."

"Okay," Bill said, only slightly interested. The surroundings made him nervous and he half-expected something out of the ordinary to happen at any moment. He didn't know what.

PickneyDaddy, however, wasn't finished yet.

"Mek me tell you somet'ing...you see inna the olden days everybody fear Honey Hole like dem fear the baddest duppy you could ah imagine. The t'ings dem wha' did ah gwan down yah only God could ah come yah an' safe. One day one preacher man name Pastor Willard did move down ah St Thomas from town an' him seh dat him ah go open up church down yah an' cleanse the place an' drive out all ah the wicked obeah an' bad spirit and convert all the heathen. We all ah laugh 'pon him, true we know dat many ah try an' many ah fail. Me seh the man nevah touch down two minute inna St Thomas before him start gwan with him bad man strain. Anyway, him build him church. Now the said church did burn down as pure bad spirit tek over the place an' if you look like Witness or one ah dem other denomination, the spirit dem would ah tek you an' mash yuh head 'gainst rock and drain out you brain fe joke.

"The man open up the place one night an' tell him daughter fe stay home that night 'cause him nuh know wha' fe expect. Him start preach an' ah galang, an' him did see one young girl inna the congregation. Bwoy is then the spirit did hol' him. You know, the man fall in love with the girl an' tek her one night after him sermon an' have him wicked way with her right deh inna the church. An' guess wha', dat same night, the whole ah the church burn down again. Preacher burn to ash, but dem nevah find the gal deh. Y'understand wha' me seh. After dat, Mr Brown build him school house where church used to be."

They arrived at Stylehut soon after, as the darkness began to set in. It deepened Bill's reluctance to go further. But it was too late. He knew that PickneyDaddy wouldn't turn back at this stage and trying to go back on his own was worse than proceeding further.

Stylehut was typical of country life in Jamaica. It had a

scattering of cheaply built houses, some with electricity and many without. Candlelight was the main source of lighting, but by far the most unsatisfactory aspect of living were the toilets: often just a hole in the ground, a short distance from the living quarters.

Bill and PickneyDaddy walked on slowly, a slight hesitation in every step. They were in Stylehut, but more importantly, they were in Honey Hole, a famed part of Stylehut where only the brave dared to roam. According to legend, so much magic was practiced in Stylehut that the grass and trees were able to trap and imprison any unfortunate soul who might wander in.

In the middle of the sandy main road stood a stand pipe, its drip-drip-dripping of water shattering the silence repetitively. This pipe would have provided most of the water to the small community, who were scattered along the winding road. Someone must have just used it, Bill thought, walking over to it and twisting the tap shut.

"You haffe aarks before you use the water y'know," a coarse voice echoed from somewhere, Bill couldn't tell where. PickneyDaddy nudged him and pointed to a scraggy looking woman peering down at them.

"You nevah hear wha' me did seh?" the woman queried from the huge rock face on top of which she stood. She was skinny and as black as a dutch pot, her head wrapped in a bright yellow turban.

"The pickney nevah use the water," PickneyDaddy announced. "He jus' turn off the tap, true smaddy did lef' it ah drip."

"Oh," the woman replied, still unsatisfied.

"You know whe' the Science man deh?" PickneyDaddy shouted up. The woman looked them both up and down. There was a smirk on her face as if she was saying, 'I know what

110

you're here for'. Then she answered, "go down so," she pointed down the winding road, "an' when you meet one ben'-up tree, tek the path an' you will find the yard in front ah you."

Before they had a chance to thank her, the woman had vanished from view, leaving PickneyDaddy and Bill perplexed as to where she had gone.

They wasted no time following the woman's instructions. From the twisted tree the path was clearly visible, but the route was dense with bushes and trees. The two pushed their way through until they saw the shack, in an acute state of disrepair. It looked as if no-one had lived in it for years, except for the small wood fire in front of the house upon which a pot was bubbling with an acrid liquid. The fumes assaulted Bill's nostrils with a painful sting.

"Me nah go in deh," Bill decided suddenly.

PickneyDaddy turned around and observed his young friend for a moment. He noticed the terror in his eyes and saw cold sweat form on his brow.

"Dat ah yuh business," PickneyDaddy replied, marching off towards the house.

For the second time since arriving at Stylehut, Bill had wanted to turn back, but, for the second time, the choice of going forward with his companion or turning back alone had left him with the conclusion that there was strength in numbers. For a moment, he thought he heard the trees around him moan with grief. Maybe it was the wind, then again, maybe it wasn't. Bill didn't stick around to find out, but quickly joined PickneyDaddy.

Even as they approached the door to the shack, Bill's mind was filled with the misgivings he had had all along. There on the door were painted signs which sent a shudder down his spine just to look at. He didn't know what they meant and didn't wish to know either. But the fact that he had never seen such signs before in his life only seemed to confirm to him that there was something evil lurking behind that wooden door.

They stood in front of the doorway for a moment, the older man turning momentarily to his younger companion with a look of anxiety. If PickneyDaddy was searching Bill's face for advice on what to do next, he was not likely to get it. There was an awkward silence between them as PickneyDaddy considered his options. He could either knock on the door or shout out their presence.

"Right now," he confessed, "me head inna confusion an' me heart inna me mout' an me stomach ah twist an' turn an' me head full up ah doubt..."

He didn't have to consider too long however, before the door opened with a long, mournful creak.

"Ah who dat?" a high-pitched woman's voice squawked from the darkness within, sending a shiver down both the visitor's spine.

"Bap, Bap send we," Pickney Daddy answered quickly and nervously. "Me is PickneyDaddy."

There was a long silence as if the woman on the other side of the door was weighing up the reply carefully. Then the door swung open. But there was no woman on the other side, only an old man staring at them through deep-set, watery eyes.

"Ah, Bap, Bap," the man acknowledged finally, in a kindly baritone. And, straightening up, he moved further towards them. "Yes, Bap, Bap ah one ole friend ah mine. If him send you, is a'right. You bettah come inside before the spirit dem ketch you."

Bill looked around immediately, half-expecting some evil spirit to pounce on them, before quickly following PickneyDaddy into the shack.

112

The interior was dim and had an eerie feel to it. Though outside a warm evening breeze lapped lazily through the trees, inside this shack it was positively chilly. Several shrunken monkey skulls hung from the ceiling with lengths of string and all around the shack bottles of every shape and size filled with liquids of every colour and description stood waiting patiently to be called upon in some service or other.

Bill gasped at the sight, PickneyDaddy merely looked quietly around. The man closed the door behind them and went towards a small round table at a corner of the shack where a candle stood. He sat down. PickneyDaddy took Massa Allen's stone from his bag and handed it to the man. He snatched it impatiently and deposited it quickly in a pouch that hung from his side. Then PickneyDaddy began to tell him of their reason for being there. He believed that obeah had been practiced on a young girl in his family. He took a small coloured bottle out of his pocket and explained that it was the water that Ella had passed that morning. He handed it over to the man. He examined it closely under the flickering flame of the candlelight, all the time nodding his head and cackling softly to himself. He agreed that Ella was sick and that obeah was behind her illness.

The man leaned over and reached in a sack under his table. He pulled out an opaque bottle and held it up in his outstretched hand. Then he uncapped it and, with the top off, brought it up to his nose and took a deep breath, inhaling as much as he could of the contents. He closed his eyes momentarily, then blinked awake again.

"Unuh mustn't frighten, y'hear," he said in a benign voice, pouring some of the thick blue content of the bottle onto his hands. He approached the senior of his two visitors, daubing the liquid on his face. PickneyDaddy shivered unintentionally as the ice-cold liquid gripped his skin.

"But wait…" PickneyDaddy said bemused, "ah nuh me the one who sick y'know," he reminded the man. The obeah man simply smiled.

"Me know," he said softly, "but which one ah we know the science? Me or unuh…?"

PickneyDaddy was still confused but decided to co-operate.

Bill felt scared, he was sure he had heard an old woman's voice when they arrived, but he had scanned every inch of the one room shack and there was nowhere for anybody to be hiding. He glanced across at PickneyDaddy and saw a concerned look on his face.

The man then reached down to the floor and placed his hand in his pouch. He produced a red cloth which he tied round his head. He quickly opened his hand and sitting snugly in the middle were three small white stones, glowing in the dimly lit room. "Come closer," he said, throwing the stones on to the table. "You see dem yah stones. When you go back home, dig a hole inna yuh yard to the north, east an' west an' bury each stone in the hole. Mek sure you cover up the hole dem back. Dat will keep the spirit dem from the yard an' protect anybody who live 'pon the land; even when you lef' the yard." His eyes shone as he explained. PickneyDaddy cupped the stones in his hand and stashed them in the ragged bag that swung freely from his shoulder. The obeah man then fingered four crosses on PickneyDaddy's face, slowly and carefully, all the time chanting and mumbling unintelligibly. Then, gradually, as he sang, he began to shake his hips with increasing speed, until he danced himself into a trance, all the time chanting louder and faster. And then, almost as suddenly as he had begun, he slumped to the floor, heaving and gulping for air, as if he were about to die from his exertions.

114

PickneyDaddy and Bill stood staring at the man on the ground. This was the second time they had witnessed such a performance, but, unlike Shepherd Allen, this man filled them with dread. They exchanged nervous glances, not knowing what to do next. Bill wanted to go, but PickneyDaddy wasn't sure.

Suddenly, out from under the table, there was a movement, so quick that they didn't quite see what it was before it was gone.

"The dyam sint'ing!" the man's voice suddenly bellowed as he struggled to his feet hastily. "Come," he grabbed PickneyDaddy by the hand, "an' help me ketch dis dyam sint'ing."

"Ketch wha' sint'ing?" PickneyDaddy asked as the man dragged him outside of the shack. Bill, who was too scared to stay inside by himself, followed them.

"Dat deh sint'ing!" the man cried, pointing a shaking finger at a small black animal scurrying away into the bushes.

It was only then that PickneyDaddy realized what it was.

"A monkey?" PickneyDaddy slapped his thigh in disbelief. He couldn't stop himself from letting out a deep laugh.

"Yes, ketch the dyam sint'ing," the man urged. Pushing a reluctant PickneyDaddy after it. But the old man refused to budge.

"Dat monkey is a spirit dem send down from Water Valley fe vex me soul," the man said.

No matter how much he pleaded with him, PickneyDaddy refused to go after the monkey and capture it. He said they had to be getting back. The obeah man sulked for a moment before handing PickneyDaddy an opaque bottle of liquid to take with him to the ailing child.

"Tek dis with you to cleanse her from the evil spirit. Hol' on to the medicine, nuh."

These were the obeah man's last words before closing his door on the outside world. PickneyDaddy smirked as he set off, following the path back to the road. Bill quickened his stride at the sound of rustling coming from the bushes on either side of the path. Had this been anywhere else, he would have concluded that the sound was due to a wild animal, or a goat, or the runaway monkey. But here in Stylehut, every unexplained sound had the possibility of having something to do with the supernatural.

"Me feel seh me did hear one duppy back ah me jus' now," he said uneasily.

"Duppy too frighten fe come out ah dis time ah night," PickneyDaddy teased. "Especially 'round yahso." He chuckled to himself, a loud and satisfied laugh.

"You mean some duppy 'fraid?"

"Oh, yes," PickneyDaddy nodded. "You mean you don't know dat duppy can 'fraid?"

"You ah joke," Bill scoffed, dismissing the suggestion.

"Hear wha'," PickneyDaddy grabbed him by the shoulder as he led him out onto the road. "One day me did stranded down ah Mount Felix, true me did ah do some runnings down deh an' t'ing…"

Bill mashed his mouth, rolled his eyes up at the velvet night sky in anticipation of one of the old man's tall stories.

"PickneyDaddy, me hear dis one already," Bill remonstrated, but PickneyDaddy denied ever telling this particular story.

"Anyhow," he continued, "me seh the night jus' draw in an' the dyam road black it black it black so 'til me could hardly see a dyam," he said, screwing up his face. "The taxi dem, me nuh know wha' did happen to dem dat deh night, true me nevah

116

see one fe all two, three hour. Two twos me hear one sound down yonder an' it ah get louder true me ah walk towards it." PickneyDaddy's face was intense as he gulped to take a breather. If anyone knew how to tell a story it was this old man who knew not only how to capture his audience's attention, but how to keep the listener in suspense—expertise he had developed over many long years of storytelling.

"When me get closer, me hear one noise like whip. Then me hear 'nuff whip ah lash like when dem use to whip the criminal dem down ah the jail house. Me head start grow, y'see, like it ah go explode. The noise get so loud me haffe cork me ears. Then me 'member: Ah Whipping Bwoy from the cattle farm."

"Whipping Bwoy?" Bill questioned.

"Yes," PickneyDaddy replied, "you nuh know Whipping Bwoy?"

Bill shrugged his shoulders.

"Cho'," PickneyDaddy mumbled, "unuh pickney nuh know life. Whipping Bwoy ah one duppy. Him did work down ah the farm an' use to work with cow an' t'ing. Him did have 'bout t'ree whip like dem ole-time cowboy. One day him use him whip an' flog one teef. The teef come back with him friend dem an' chop up Whipping Bwoy mince. From dem time, dem seh him walk up an' down ah night time ah flash him whip dem."

"So wha'ppen, PickneyDaddy?" Bill asked impatiently.

"Well," he continued, "me reach one spot an' all me can hear was a whip ah lash from all direction. Me smell one stink smell like when man mingle with cow an' nuh wash fe all a week. Two twos me hear one howling an' me head start growl again. True it dark me couldn't see a t'ing, but me did know Whipping Bwoy did deh 'bout deh. Me start chant some Psalms y'see, an' when me done me tek foot down the road—

117

fast! Me seh the dyam Whipping Bwoy deh back ah me ah flash him t'ings. Me inna so much haste dat me stumble an' fall an' jus' close me eyes an' ah wait fe Whipping Bwoy fe tek me from the eart'. Me feel one lash ah the whip 'cross me neckback an' me close me eye tight an' pray him nuh chew me bones fe joke.

"Suddenly me hear one piece ah thunder an' lightning explode above me head. Me open me eye dem wide an' me could see Whipping Bwoy ah bend over me fe lick out me life. The thunder roll again an' me hear one crashing noise come from one cliff top. When me tek a stock an' open me eye, me see two eyeballs ah blaze with fire."

"Wha' you ah talk 'bout, PickneyDaddy?" Bill interrupted. "Not'n nuh gwan so."

"You feel so," PickneyDaddy replied, stopping in the middle of the road to ponder Bill's disbelief. "You hear 'bout Rolling Calf, bwoy?" he asked.

Bill nodded his head as his eyes widened with the mention of the name.

"Me seh Rolling Calf ah tear down the cliff side an' ah come directly towards me. The two eyes dem ah spit fire, an' the chain back ah it jus' ah rattle an' ah mek 'nuff noise fe wake the whole parish. All me hear is Whipping Bwoy ah flash him whip until him disappear. Yes," PickneyDaddy nodded slowly, "the dyam sump'n nuh tek foot an' gone an' lef' me to the mercy ah the Rolling Calf. Bwoy, me nevah know me could ah run so fast, but the nex' t'ing me know me deh back ah me yard, fast asleep."

PickneyDaddy roared with laughter at the unexpected twist in his story's conclusion. He laughed so loud that tears came to his eyes and he had to hold his stomach in pain. Bill realized that he had been had and just as he was about to lighten up, two blazing red bull's eyes appeared suddenly out of the dark night, heading for them at speed.

"Rolling Calf!" Bill screamed as he froze to the spot. The bull's eyes were still coming towards them rapidly. They could hear a clanging noise and a roar which penetrated the night air.

"PickneyDaddy, do sump'n nuh!" Bill cried, his body shaking with fear.

PickneyDaddy stepped out into the middle of the road and waved his arms in the air.

"Dat nah do not'n!" Bill screamed. "You nuh see the t'ing ah come fe nyam we fe food!"

PickneyDaddy simply laughed some more. In another moment, the bull's eyes seemed to have slowed down and were coming to a halt. It was only then that Bill realized that they had already walked all the way back to Duppy Bridge.

"You ah go DeepWell?" PickneyDaddy asked as the taxi's engine shook, rattled and stuttered to a halt. "Jump in nuh," the taxi driver replied. PickneyDaddy glanced at Bill, who was breathing more easily now, and pushed him into the half-empty taxi, where they sat back and reflected on their Stylehut adventures. "You haffe stop tell dem story y'know, PickneyDaddy," Bill giggled, seeing the funny side of things now. "Of course," PickneyDaddy agreed. "Me story dem too hot fe handle."

Bill turned his head and watched through the taxi's rear window as Duppy Bridge disappeared in the distance. "Bwoy," the taxi man sighed with relief. "You see when it come to night time..." he paused, spluttered, and coughed violently, " 'nuff people waan go ah dem side deh. Me a eediat? Or ah money me waan?" He shrugged his shoulders and sped off into the night.

EIGHT
Tings Come Up To Bump

The taxi screeched to a halt on the big bend in the road outside Ole Miller's place, and Bill tried to coax the taxi man to drive right up to their house, a little bit further, but to no avail.

"Me not yuh personal driver yah," he retorted as the doors slammed shut and he spun his steering wheel full circle for the u-turn. "Unuh lucky me carry unuh dis far." His blunt manner was only matched by the abruptness of his departure as, wheel-spinning into the distance, the car zoomed out of sight in the direction it came from.

PickneyDaddy lamented the old days, when a taxi driver had manners, as they made their way to the house.

Jim had come home from the rum bar and was now at his daughter's side, beside his wife, when the bedroom door swung open.

"See it yah!" PickneyDaddy cried out, as he waved the obeah man's bottle in front of him.

Mom Butler looked away nervously.

"Wha' dat?" Jim asked.

120

"Ah the medicine for Ella," PickneyDaddy announced proudly. "She haffe get better nuh."

Jim held out his hand to examine the bottle. PickneyDaddy handed it over to him and he took it in his hand, studying it closely. He pulled out the cork and inhaled deeply. The fumes from the liquid inside were so strong that they burned his nostrils. He turned his head away hurriedly.

"Blouse an' skirt! What happen, you waan kill me daughter? Whe' you get dis?"

"Ah from one man down ah Stylehut."

"Stylehut!"

"Yeah man... Mom Butler tell me fe..."

"STYLEHUT!!" Jim couldn't believe what he was hearing. He turned to his wife for an explanation, but she simply turned away.

"Ah so me seh," PickneyDaddy confirmed.

Jim was breathing heavily. He could think of plenty of things to say to PickneyDaddy, but none of them were without curses. He threw the bottle back at the old man as if it had scalded his hand. Then he turned to his wife.

"Is wha' you ah deal with?" he asked her with bitterness. "You ah send fe obeah worker nuh? Is wha' the blouse an' skirt you ah deal with?"

Mom Butler remained with her head turned away from her husband. She hadn't expected him home so soon. If he hadn't been turfed out of the rum bar, she would have been able to give Ella some of the medicine to make sure that she got better, instead of just relying on the 'cleansing' of a healer.

"ANSWER ME 'OOMAN!" Jim cried out in frustration.

Mom Butler turned around and looked her husband in the eye. She was about to say something, when a tiny voice spoke softly.

121

"Mom…? Dada…?"

All eyes turned to the bed where Ella was opening sleepy eyes. She lay perfectly still.

"You a'right now. The bad spirit dem gone," Mom Butler assured her with a warm smile.

"El'…" her father said, rushing over to her and holding her hand.

"Dada… me win, Dada," she said quietly.

"Win wha'?" Jim asked, a quizzical look on his face.

"The big race, Dada. The one ah school."

Jim Butler smiled and congratulated her. He looked around at the others in the room and saw three warm, happy faces. He had forgotten all about the race his daughter had been so much looking forward to participating in. But it was the first thing that registered in Ella's mind when she finally awakened from her state of unconsciousness. She seemed like the old Ella and Jim hoped she was back to stay.

"So, wha'ppen inna the race?" Jim asked with a twinkle in his eye, "an' you sure you nevah come second place?"

"Cho'," Ella murmured with a wry smile on her face. "Second ah fe losers."

"You nuh see't?" Jim laughed out loud. He laughed so loud, he was soon coughing and spluttering. "Ahh," he sighed, regaining control of his breathing, "don't mek me do dat again, El."

Every bit the proud father, he congratulated his daughter as she ran over the events that had led to her victory, including the fact that she'd been suffering in pain as she ran.

"You can run race an' win, but fe do somet'ing fe me tek all day," Mom Butler added, stroking her daughter's head, smiling.

"Nuh mind Mom," Jim joked, "bettah you run an' do

somet'ing good, than run an' do it bad."

Ella felt great. She was being fussed over by her family like never before. The three people she loved the most were at her bedside and they seemed to be one happy family again. She fell asleep, a look of contentment on her face.

Jim Butler still had some serious business to discuss with his wife. He took the opportunity to confront her while Ella was resting.

"Me can't believe you send fe a obeah worker," he told her.

Mom Butler looked him straight in the eye. "Me will try anyt'ing fe mek me daughter well."

"Yes Mom, but the obeah…you know how it mash up t'ings inna yuh family."

Mom Butler knew only too well. She nodded. But that wasn't the point. She thought that Ella was going to die and she didn't have as much faith in Shepherd Allen's healing process.

Jim continued. "Me believe ah obeah work kill yuh mammy. An' you know yuh faada believe it. Dat's why him nah leave an inch of him land fe yuh sister when him pass away."

Painful memories filled Grace's head. Memories of that strict and upright figure, her father, who had brought her up to work hard and honestly and to praise the Lord on a Sunday. 'Marry fe love an' work fe money,' her father was always fond of telling his daughter. And 'man build house, but woman make the home'. He was proud and took care of his wife and daughter as well as any man in the area. But he had always longed for a son and when Jim Butler approached him to ask for his daughter's hand in marriage, Ole Jackson quickly took to the young man from Seaport, who reminded him of himself at that age. In fact, after the marriage Ole Jackson didn't have to worry about farming any more, as, between them, Jim and his new bride, Grace, were able to take care of everything. Ole Jackson and his wife could enjoy their middle-age and the old man even started talking of Jim as his natural heir.

Then one rainy night, the messenger of doom knocked on their door loudly and rapidly. Mistress Jackson, Grace's mother, opened the door. Before her on the verandah, stood a bedraggled woman, soaked to the skin by the rain. With her was a beautiful young girl, her daughter. The woman looked at Mistress Jackson with a sneer and asked if her husband was at home. Mom Butler's mother had no reason to be suspicious because the woman was known to her—Mona Roberts rented a little piece of land from the Jacksons down by Flatgrass and lived there with her daughter Marian—but there was something about the way she sneered that made Mistress Jackson suspicious and she demanded to know why Mona wanted to see her husband. A quarrel ensued between the two women with Mona accusing Mistress Jackson of sticking her nose too much in other people's affairs while Mistress Jackson refused to even call her husband. Finally, Mona blurted it out, "Tell yuh husband dat him pickney need feeding…all ah dem, not just one."

At first Mistress Jackson didn't comprehend. But that was just for a short moment, for as her eyes wandered towards Mona's daughter, it suddenly dawned on her; the eyes, the mouth, that proud look on her face, Marian and Grace shared so many similarities. And, as it dawned on her, Mistress Jackson's safe world collapsed around her. As it did, so did her heart.

"Oh lawd!" she gasped, as her legs gave way. She reached out to steady herself, but it was too late.

Even before Ole Jackson made it out to the verandah to see what all the commotion was about, Mistress Jackson had suffered a massive stroke, from which she would never fully recover.

Even though she could not communicate, Dr Gardener had said that she still had feelings and he was sure that she was aware of everything and everyone around her. No amount of healing helped either. Shepherd Allen cleansed her and did all he could for her, but Mistress Jackson failed to respond. It was then that Shepherd Allen informed Ole Jackson of the fact that he had 'seen somet'ing' hanging over his wife's head, and advised him that obeah work was at play.

For the next twelve months, Ole Jackson cursed his mistress for having destroyed his family through 'science'. Instead of easing into retirement, the rest of his life would be spent nursing his wife as she lay motionless in bed—feeding her, washing her and caring for her every need—or taking her for long walks in the hillsides in the primitive wheelchair his son-in-law had constructed out of wood and a couple of old bicycle tyres. Only the fact that he would be making his other daughter, Marian, homeless at the same time stopped him from evicting Mona.

At the same time, she grew to hate the man with whom she had lain and for whom she had borne a child. She had remained quiet for seventeen years as the 'outside woman'. She hadn't complained when weeks went by without her Marian seeing her father. She hadn't protested when she and her daughter had to struggle to survive while Ole Jackson's other family lived in comfort. They lived in a proper house, not a shack like she and Marian, and they farmed enough food to make a small profit from their produce. Mona never said a word when she saw her daughter's half-sister parading in new

125

clothes, while she had little more than rags to offer Marian. The only assistance he gave them was to allow them to live rent free, unbeknown to his wife. She had accepted it all in the belief that in death Ole Jackson would treat his daughters equally and divide his land between them. That was what he had always said. Until, that is, this fancy young man had come from Seaport and married Grace Jackson.

She knew what she was doing when she arrived at the Jackson's house on that fateful day. She, like everybody else, had heard the local gossip of how Ole Jackson was so endeared to his son-in-law that he intended to leave all his land to him and his daughter. She couldn't believe how easily he had forgotten his younger child. She had trudged through the rainstorm with her daughter to stake Marian's claim, in front of all of the Jacksons. But everything had backfired. In the last year Ole Jackson had cut her out of his life, and now she feared that he would cut Marian out of her legacy once and for all.

The reason she went down to the bridge at Roaring River was to waylay Ole Jackson. He often pushed his paralyzed wife's chair along that route and she was bound to meet him. Mona returned to the bridge for four days in a row before he showed up. She wasn't in an angry mood, she just wanted him to understand his responsibilities towards the child she had born him. But Ole Jackson was furious when he saw her, accusing her of lying in wait for him. Nobody really knows what followed, but it took another week for all three bodies to be found, much further down river.

As it was her father's wish, Mom Butler had reluctantly allowed her half-sister Marian to continue living on the land. Even after Marian subsequently married Robert Johnson and moved half his family there.

Later that night PickneyDaddy burst back into the Butler home, looking flustered and out of breath.

"You wake?" he called out loudly, standing in the hallway, his breath coming and going in spurts.

Jim was first out of the room, followed by Bill, then Ella, with Mom Butler making up the rear. Jim nodded wearily and PickneyDaddy continued. "Me have some terrible news. Dat deh Swinger killer gone with a nex' life!"

"You did hear seh a nex' killing happen?"

Bill and Ella looked at each other, completely puzzled and confused.

"Yes," PickneyDaddy continued. "The bwoy dem call Maaga Dawg, dem find him rope up ah one tree inna gully down ah Yallahs Bay. The tree did use fe one swing fe the children dem."

The whole family turned and looked at the old man who was shaking and sweating as he spoke. They could see he was scared.

"Wha' you ah seh, ole man?" Mom Butler asked as she continued to tend to her husband.

"You nevah hear wha' me did seh?" PickneyDaddy shouted hysterically. "Dem find one dead bwoy down ah the cross road...you see how yuh lucky, Ella?" A bead of sweat trickled down his forehead.

"How yuh mean?" Ella queried with a puzzled look.

"Bwoy, you waan see, dem find the Walker bwoy 'tone cold, the bwoy spirit lick outta him like the rest!"

"You mean Bubsy?" Ella cried, jumping off her seat, her eyes already filling with tears. From the expression on his face, Bill was also shocked by the news, but he said nothing.

"Lawd have mercy. You mean the crossroad down so?"

Mom Butler queried with alarm.

PickneyDaddy nodded. "Bwoy, it ah get close to we yah."

"Bubsy was in my class, Mom," Ella sobbed.

"Nuh min' yaar, dear," Mom Butler said, stroking her daughter's head sympathetically, "dem will ketch the brute wha' do this, an' the Lawd who watches over all ah we ah go pass him own judgment when the right time come. 'Cause nuh care how smaddy ah gwan bad, sinting deh fe spokes him wheel."

That was hardly enough to reassure Ella. After all, Bubsy disappeared during the Big Race, it could so easily have been her.

"Ketch him? Cho'!" PickneyDaddy chimed. "Dem nah ketch dat deh killer."

Then the old man started to describe the state of the body when it was found but Mrs Butler stopped him cold.

"Look now, nuh bother come frighten up me pickney dem."

She rebuked the old man before turfing him out of their home. Then, turning to Bill and Ella, she said, "unuh pickney haffe careful how you walk ah road, true 'nuff mad man deh 'bout yah. You shake man hand but you nuh shake dem heart."

There was an uneasy silence in the house as PickneyDaddy's revelations began to sink in deep. Jim was in quiet contemplation, wondering how far this thing would continue and what he should do to protect his family and those he loved from this killer who seemed not to discriminate in his choice of victims.

Mom Butler was also thinking, and considering what option she had open to herself if she was confronted by the killer on a quiet afternoon when she was at home alone. She didn't really believe that she would be as vulnerable as all his other victims and had enough faith in her own strength to see her through to survival.

Bill was thinking about how nothing could happen to him, he was young and strong and could defend himself when the time called for it, but he believed the likelihood would be that he **could be** called upon to defend his sister from the clutches of the maniac. Ella, meanwhile, was thinking that there was no way the killer could catch her. She was that sure and confident about her speed, but what of Bill? He was so slow and sluggish. How would she save her brother from the killer if the occasion called for it?

"PickneyDaddy well 'fraid," Bill commented. "Bwoy, imagine! Yuh coulda run into the killer inna the race, Ella."

His sister didn't answer. On the table in front of her stood the trophy, a glorious token of her achievement, but she stared past it, out into the front yard.

A few days later, Ella had made a complete recovery. Climbing out of bed, she went into the yard to have a wash then changed into a clean dress. It was dawn and she had been sleeping since early the previous morning. She had slept so much she felt exhausted and now wanted some fresh air. She went out onto the verandah and found Bill standing there, staring apprehensively up at the sky. The last few days hadn't been easy for him and it showed on his face. He seemed somehow older and wiser.

"El," he said, turning to greet his sister with a huge smile, "you feel bettah?"

She nodded with a loud yawn. Then she stretched out with her arms to activate muscles which had remained dormant for too long.

"You shouldn't be outta yuh bed, y'know…"

"Me feel fine," Ella replied.

"It look like Mom an' Dad doin' fine too," Bill grinned. He was glad that his parents' relationship seemed to be improving but he still felt awkward with his father. It was the first time in ages that their family were united. He wondered if it would last. Would his father's drinking continue? For the moment, he could only guess at that.

Ella drew breath and her heart started to gallop. "Me feel seh ah Ole Miller ah do dem t'ings y'know," she said, her voice trembling. "Ole Miller mussa do it," she insisted.

"How dat?" Bill yawned, hardly taking his sister seriously, his mind already on his warm bed and an early night's sleep. He was much too tired to be playing detectives with his sister.

"Come on, Bill," Ella coaxed. She wanted her brother to start thinking of the possibilities of Ole Miller being the killer. She told him about the 'travelling' she had done while she was still delirious. But Bill wasn't as convinced that her dreams about the Ole Miller house were significant.

"Me nuh understand," Bill said.

"It's easy," Ella concluded. "It all tie up. The man mussi the Devil 'cause him did drive him mudda mad and mussa practice the evil inna the house."

Bill turned and looked at his sister as if she were mad, and if Ole Miller was to reveal himself before them now, he would probably hand his sister over to him if it meant that he would get a bit of peace and quiet.

"Yeah," she continued, "him daddy did all dead mysteriously about thirty years ago an' dat ah the same time the birdfoot killer deh ah butcher all the people dem. Bwoy..." Ella marvelled at her own powers of deduction, "me well an' truly find out the trut'."

"Ella, yuh mad!" Bill shouted. "What proof yuh have?"

130

"Bill, dat's why me haffe find out if him inna the yard. Dat deh place have all the answers an' me mus' find out."

"Bwoy, me tired, y'know, an' me waan go ah me bed. We nuh have no time fe dat." Bill yawned again, this time loudly and prolonged.

"You still 'fraid ah Ole Miller, Bill?" Ella asked, as they turned to go back in the house.

"Ah who seh dat? Me nuh 'fraid ah dat ole man," Bill chuckled.

Ella teased some more. Her brother was terrified and she knew it, she said. She could see it in his eyes and what's more there was a trickle of sweat forming on his brow which gave the game away. Bill wiped the sweat off hurriedly with the back of his hand and blamed it on the early evening humidity.

"No, me nuh 'fraid," Bill said once again, "but me know seh somet'ing strange happen inna dat house…"

Ella listened keenly, her vivid imagination hanging on every word.

"PickneyDaddy tell me one time 'bout it. Ole Miller him did suppose fe get married one day, back in dem times…"

"Dat deh monster did ah go marry?" Ella cringed as if the thought was just too horrible to imagine.

"Hol' on nuh, me nuh tell the story yet…like me seh, Ole Miller suppose fe get married one day an' the t'ing did happen. But 'pon him wedding night deh him an' him bride did ah ramp an' t'ing an' when him argue Ole Miller slip an' pitch her down the stairs. She fall bad an' she pop her neck. PickneyDaddy tell me seh Ole Miller blame himself an', true the grief get heavy, him all ah pitch himself inna the grave fe stay with her. Dem haffe get ten strong man fe hol' him down while dem throw the dutty 'pon the casket. After dat me hear seh her family did go fe look 'pon the grave one day and dem

131

find the grave dig up an' empty. Dem search the whole ah the parish, but you know wha'?"

Bill paused to heighten the suspension. Mesmerized, Ella shrugged her shoulders, "Me nuh know."

"Bwoy," Bill said exageratedly, "the only place dem nevah search was Ole Miller's house where she sitting perch up inna chair with the wedding hat an' dress an' every dyam t'ing. Maggots all ah bury through the eyeball and the woman teet 'kin it coming like day ghost."

"Ah lie you ah tell," Ella cried, her eyes wide with fear.

"Yeah? Ah so you feel?" Bill said.

Just then, Mom Butler poked her head out of their bedroom window.

"So you ah wake, child?"

Ella nodded. She told her mother that she felt fresh and well.

"So wha' ah gwan?"

"Mom," Bill said, still grinning, "Ella t'ink seh Ole Miller ah the killer."

"Who talk so?"

"Me nuh know, y'know, jus' ah feeling me have," Ella summed up.

"Well," Mom Butler began, "unuh should lef' him alone. You play with dog dem lick yuh mouth, you sleep with dog, you ketch him flea."

"You mean Ole Miller definitely alive?" Ella asked.

"Of course," Mom Butler replied. "The man jus' keep himself to himself. Cockroach nah business ah fowl yard."

This, at last, was confirmation that it was a living man rather than a duppy residing in the big house at the bend in the road. Ella swapped looks with Bill who shrugged his shoulders with an upwards roll of his eyes.

132

Ella sat sandwiched between Bill and her father at Bubsy's funeral service, held in the same classroom which Bubsy, in life, did his best to avoid coming to. Today, the classroom was packed to the brim. Mom Butler had decided not to go. She hated funerals and only attended if it was a family member. Sister Ivy had asked for her when they first arrived and Ella had made the appropriate excuses for Mom Butler's absence before taking a seat.

The preacher, a serious-looking, huge mountain of a man, was sweating profusely in the heat and paused in his sermon to wipe his brow with a handkerchief and take a sip from a can of Red Stripe. Pastor Stephenson liked Red Stripe. "We all haffe march to the promised land..." he continued. Pastor Stephenson was in fine form. This was the second funeral service he was officiating for the day. He had earlier presided over the funeral of Robert Johnson and was by now getting a feel for how to manipulate his service so as to touch his listeners where it hurt the most. This was his finest hour and he didn't intend to waste it. Like the consummate preacher he was, he had the mourners hanging on his every word, his every turn of phrase.

As Ella was casting yet another glance behind her at the silent mourners assembled, her eyes locked onto a thin man who sat isolated at the back of the room. She hadn't noticed him before and she didn't recognize him. It was a reasonably small community and whoever you didn't know you at least recognized. The man looked strange and somehow out of place. Ella couldn't tell how old he was, but he was old enough to be her grandfather and there was something about him, something about his dark, inexpressive mask of a face. No matter how she tried, Ella couldn't actually see the man's eyes, which were lowered as if in silent prayer.

The man suddenly looked up and two deep gleaming eyes bore into Ella's inquisitive gaze. She spun around quickly, feeling flustered and trembling visibly.

"Wha' wrong?" Bill whispered to her, noticing her distress.

Ella didn't answer.

From the pulpit, Pastor Stephenson was admonishing those youngsters present for believing that they would live for ever. "Who told you so?" he asked rhetorically, making sure that now he had these young ears listening to him for once, he would do everything in his power to put the fear of God into them. Bubsy's 'girlfriend', Jaqueline, burst out crying as Pastor Stephenson reminded them that Bubsy didn't know that he would be called to meet his maker so soon.

"Wha'ppen to you?" Bill asked again, nudging his sister with his elbow.

"Ole Miller deh yah," Ella whispered back, keeping her head straight and bowed.

"Don't be stupid," Bill answered, giggling at the suggestion. "Ole Miller would ah frighten off all the people dem, or nyam dem fe food."

"Me serious," Ella responded agitatedly. "Look back so and see if you see one half-dead man who look like duppy."

As the congregation rose to sing the next hymn, Bill stole a quick glance back but could see no-one matching the description Ella had given him.

"Cho'," he nudged his sister with his elbow again, "you ah try fe scare me. You see anyone deh?"

Ella swirled around and saw the chair where the man had previously sat, now empty. She looked at Bill and then away. She hadn't imagined it. He had been there. But where had he

134

gone?

The service seemed to gain pace from then on, as family member after family member visited the alter to pour out their tribute to Bubsy. Ella refused to take part in the procession filing past the body at the end of the service. She had only ever seen one dead body and wanted to keep it that way.

"You too stupid!" Bill blasted Ella as they left the church.

"Don't call yuh sister stupid," Jim whispered to Bill. "Is not everybody like the dead."

"Yeah me know," Bill retorted. "But ah the gal friend an' she nah see him again." He pushed out his mouth and continued to follow the crowd.

Ella's feet were hurting her as they left the church. This had much to do with the shoes she wore, which were uncomfortably tight at the best of times and had been squeezing her right through the service. She rarely wore shoes and the short walk to the burial place seemed to take forever.

Marian Johnson suddenly appeared right behind Jim Butler as people were starting to gather around the graveside. At first her presence startled him. After their last confrontation he was ready for anything. But once he had satisfied himself that she wasn't wielding a deadly weapon and that her brothers-in-law, Kai and Ivan, were nowhere around, he relaxed—a little.

"I realize I shoulda aarks yuh first if dat is a'right fe me bury Robert body 'pon yuh land?" she asked sarcastically as fresh tears began to roll down her cheeks.

"Bwoy," Jim began, stealing a quick look at Ella and Bill who stood innocently at his side, "me nevah even t'ink ah dat deh t'ing, y'know." He watched gingerly for Marian's reaction, but it didn't come. Instead, Syd Johnson joined her. Syd's face wasn't sad. He wore an evil smile and gazed into Bill's eyes in a provocative manner.

Jim cleared his throat and looked over at the pick-up truck by the roadside on which Robert Johnson's casket had been loaded.

"Is a'right, Marian," Jim confirmed, "you can bury him 'pon the land. You nevah expect me fe seh no?"

Marian's face creased with relief, and a slight smile crept across it. But before she could comment a voice from the crowd called, "Marian, come." It was Kai, who from the look on his face still wanted to fight Jim, any place, any time.

Jim watched Marian disappear into the swelling crowd. The burial proper over with, everyone started out to the traditional post-funeral food and drink at the house of Bubsy's grieving parents, who were determined to give their son a 'good sen'off', no matter what the circumstances and their own financial restraints. The fires which roasted the breadfruits and fried fish generated an intense heat that added to the already scorching temperature of the day. No-one seemed to mind though, as laughter and joy replaced the sobbing and grief of the burial.

Morning blended smoothly into afternoon and then evening and the number of people began to dwindle. Soon, only the domino contingent remained.

Jim had left some time ago. He'd had a lot to drink and had staggered home to sleep it off. Bill and Ella had remained, mingling with the other children, but there now seemed little to hang around for as the day slowed to a halt. The remaining children soon left, anxious to get home before it got dark; Bill and Ella decided to do the same. They were so tired they took a short cut which found them wandering through the Johnsons' grounds as they headed for home.

"Wha' you ah do here so?" snarled Syd Johnson, appearing suddenly from out of the shadows. He was still wearing his black suit, but he'd loosened his tie and his shirt now hung out of his trousers.

"Ease up nuh!" Bill raised his voice to try to quell Syd's threatening approach.

"Wha' you mean? How you can show yuh face when yuh faada done kill off me faada?" he spat venomously.

"Bwoy, wha' you ah talk 'bout?" Bill asked agitatedly as his face lined with anger. "You nuh hear, is a duppy kill yuh faada?"

Ella tugged at Bill's jacket in an attempt to make him forget about Syd and come home with her.

"Lef' me, El," Bill snapped, pushing Ella's arm away. "Dis bwoy ah gwan with too much slackness." And he stepped towards Syd.

"Syd, come yah!" Marian's loud cry ripped through the air. From the sound of his mother's voice, Syd could hear that she wasn't in a good mood. He had no intention of having his ears pulled by her in front of the 'enemy' so he took the opportunity to run off, away from both Bill and his mother.

"Me sorry," Marian apologised, as she walked towards the Butler children. She sniffed and cleared her throat. "Dat bwoy nah hear when you talk to him. Me haffe drop some licks inna him 'kin fe mek him understand wha' me ah seh." She looked drawn. The day had obviously taken its toll on her.

"Is a'right, Mistress Johnson," Ella replied, "Syd jus' upset."

"Yeah," Bill agreed, "him harmless."

Marian smiled and nodded her head in acknowledgment.

"Is hard with all dis t'ing ah gwan. Me feel seh me ah sink," she said looking glum again.

"Nuh worry," Ella squeaked. "If you need anyt'ing jus' come an' aarks." Taking those words as a comfort, Marian left them. Ella watched as she walked back up to her house.

"Bwoy, she in a bad way, don't it?" Bill said, setting off briskly for home. He was keen to get back now, and didn't want Syd or any duppies jumping out on them again.

"Wait nuh!" Ella called. "Wha' the hurry?"

"Yuh mussi nah waan sleep but me too tired fe ramp now, El."

"Nuh leave me yah!" Ella cried, running to catch up with him. "Smaddy might come an' tek me 'way."

Bill stopped quickly. In his haste he'd forgotten the killer and had been ready to leave his sister to make her own way home as he had done on many other occasions. But all the children in the area had been expressly forbidden to be out on their own since Bubsy's death. "Me nuh have no time fe dis, El."

"Hey, Bill, me feel seh dat man who did deh ah the church mussa Ole Miller."

"You mad. Whoever you t'ink you see, it wasn't Ole Miller," Bill countered. "Dat deh man lock up inna him cellar."

"Naa," Ella responded. "Me seh Ole Miller free an' him did murder Robert Johnson."

"Cho'. It nuh matter. We bettah hurry home true one maniac deh 'bout an' we nuh waan be nex'."

The two walked silently on.

They soon came to Ella's Swinging Tree, which hung limply, swaying slightly in the soft breeze.

"One minute, Bill," Ella said as she jumped onto the swing and launched herself off.

"We nuh have no time fe dis," Bill said.

"Hold on," Ella pleaded, "me nuh swing fe a while."

"You know, El," Bill began, "dis murder business ah nuh joke. Me mean it coming like dem nah ketch the Swinger."

He had a serious look on his face. The murders were getting

much too near.

"Is wha' wrong with you?" Ella asked as she dragged her feet in the dirt to stop the swing.

"Not'n nuh wrong with me, El, but the killer ah get closer an' closer. You mustn't walk about on yuh own inna the bush until dem ketch the brute."

Ella smiled at her brother's concern. As much as she wanted to be treated as an adult, she had to admit that she truly enjoyed having an older brother to care and think about her. She leaned forward to kiss him on the cheek. She didn't know why, it just felt like the right thing. Bill looked away shyly. He wasn't expecting that.

"There's not much ah dat going on with Dada an' Mom," Bill said.

"Yeah," Ella agreed. It had been so long since she last saw her mother and father embrace that she couldn't remember how long. "You feel t'ings will evah be the same again?" she asked, looking serious.

"Me don't know, El. Dada seem to have too much drink too often so him more drunk than not. How you expect Mom fe deal with dat situation day after day? You would ah like fe go through dat everyday?"

"Bill," Ella began, "you mustn't be too hard on Dada. You know Mom still ah blame him fe Little Jakie an' him must feel it too."

If Ella had expected her brother to mellow his hard feelings for his dad she would have to wait until another time. It wasn't about to happen immediately.

"Cho, you would ah seh dat. You know Dada like you, so you can't see the wrong him ah do," Bill said tersely.

"Naa, Bill, yuh wrong. Dada jus' need some love. Dat's all him need fe stop drink and you will see everyt'ing going be a'right," Ella smiled, wanting to desperately believe what she was saying.

"Yeah, it would be nice to see t'ings get back to how dem was before Little Jakie gone." Little Jakie's name sobered both of their moods, as it always did. The two siblings looked at each other uneasily for a few moments, before Ella decided to change the subject.

"Come on, yuh wan' hurry home or wha'?"

"Ella! Yuh too fast." He tried to catch her up, but she'd disappeared.

"Ella," Bill listened keenly as his own voice bounced back to him. "Ella!"

"Boo!" Ella pounced on him from behind a tree.

Bill jumped. "Cho'! You haffe do somet'ing so stupid?"

He looked up to see PickneyDaddy's silhouette walking towards them from the direction of the setting sun, as he got closer they could see his forehead was shining with sweat.

"Wha' unuh pickney up to?" he demanded. "Unuh nuh have not'n bettah fe do?"

"Bwoy, you know we get kind ah freak-out true dis swing-business." said Bill.

"Me know," PickneyDaddy responded tentatively. "Y'know," he placed one arm around Ella's shoulder, the other around Bill's, "there was only one time me did 'fraid like dis."

Bill rolled his eyes upwards as PickneyDaddy began recounting one of his famous duppy stories. Once he got started he didn't know when to stop.

"No, no, me nuh like talk 'bout duppy more than so, but lawd, dat night deh was ah night…

"Me an' one ah me friend, Deacon, jus' come outta Bath Fountain an' ah rest up little distance from deh 'pon some dutty. Deacon seh him hear one pickney cry, so we tek foot

140

down ah gully. Two twos we come to one little pen-aarf place where one fire ah burn strong an' fierce. We see one ole dry up woman with her foot all mildew ah look 'pon we from her yard before she come out fe greet we. Anyhow, we did ah talk an' talk an' we mention the pickney wha' we did hear a bawl, but the woman seh no pickney live deh, nor nowhere near deh.

"She offer we ah drink but true the stink wha' ah come from her an' the general nasty way the place did fix, we seh we can't stay, true we did have 'nuff t'ings fe do. As we 'bout fe turn an' walk 'way from the place, me eyes did ketch somet'ing strange. On one washing line dat extend from one coconut tree to a nex', me could see 'bout four or five t'ings dat coming like dolly wha' pickney play with. Dem jus' did string up, upside down.

"Well, when me aarks the woman wha' she have with dolly at her age, she start get vex an' upset. Me seh to her, 'how you have dolly an' you nuh have no pickney, and furthermore, the t'ing dem ah drip water like you jus' wash dem?' Me seh the woman a rail up 'pon me an' all ah start fe curse me like me ah pickney under her. Me should ah galang 'bout me business, but me get suspicious now an' start walk towards the dolly dem. The woman start bawl an' seh me ah go teef her dolly dem an' she ah go call solgie 'pon me…" PickneyDaddy paused, as if remembering. "Me jus' brush 'way the woman an' she drop 'pon the ground. Deacon jus' look 'pon her an' follow me. Bwoy, me tell you seh me nevah experience somet'ing like dis before. Dem nevah did dolly wha' did hook up 'pon the line— ah real pickney. The dyam woman ah vampire an' the pickney dem shrivel up. All dem eye dem ah pop out an' blood jus' ah drain from dem little body from dem mout', nose, ears, every dyam where. It coming like the woman did drain dem whole body ah blood, an' left the skin an' bones fe dry out. Ah shock,

141

ah shock, ah shock, so 'til me couldn't even speak a word to Deacon, who if you nevah know ah black man, you would ah swear blind him white. One piece ah 'fraid lick we, y'see. When we turn 'round an' look 'pon the woman, all she do is stare back an' ah giggle to herself like we ah run joke with her.

"Me go fe pick up somet'ing fe lick her down, but me couldn't move. Deacon all jus' freeze up an' ah pray seh him ah dream. Suddenly the woman start shake..." and PickneyDaddy unlatched himself from Bill and Ella, starting to shake as if to illustrate the point.

"Yes," he went on, "she start shake so 'til me did feel her whole body ah go explode. Me look 'pon Deacon, an' him look 'pon me. We did waan tek foot but it coming like the woman have we under her spell. Bwoy, but wha' did happen next, me nah forget fe the rest ah me life." He took a breath as Bill and Ella urged him to continue. "The woman jus' ah shake an' ah gwan until the woman skin fall off her body!"

Bill and Ella stopped in their tracks. "Not'n nuh gwan so," Bill scoffed, trying hard to hide his real fear.

"No?" PickneyDaddy asked provocatively, "you bettah hear wha' me ah seh, 'cause if you see wha' me jus' describe—run! Anyhow, the skin jus' drop off clean an' lay 'pon the ground ah squirm an' ah dance like it did have maggot inna it. We so shock dat we couldn't even look 'pon the woman, but, is we luck dat she jus' step outta the pile ah skin an' ah start walk toward we.

"When me look 'pon dat woman, you could see the blood jus' ah pump round her body through the veins dem. The ole woman did black, blue, red, green, every colour you could ah t'ink 'pon, she was it, an' she slimy. All some sticky sint'ing did ah drip from her flesh an' ah mek puddle 'pon the ground. Anyway, me did ah tell Deacon fe come, but the dyam fool man him couldn't move. Me all ah pull him two grain ah hair 'pon him arm, but him dead to the world. The woman she ah get closer an' uglier an' bloodier. When me tek a stock, me realize ah who—Ole Hige. 'Deacon,' me seh, 'Ah Ole Hige.' 'Ah who you call so?' Deacon ah aarks me y'know before the man come, him ah aarks stupid question. 'Ah who?' me seh. 'Ole Hige ah one ole woman who tek off her skin an' suck yuh blood until yuh life gone.'

"Deacon up 'til now still can't move, an' Ole Hige hol' him you see an' when she hol' him, her hand jus' burn into him flesh. Her tongue jus' lash out her head an' sink inna poor Deacon eye an' me see it drop out an' roll 'pon the ground before she step 'pon it an' it quash an' spurt out everywhere.

"Deacon jus' ah scream an' ah scream. Ole Hige jus' start suck out the man blood you see an' all me could ah see is Deacon body ah wither 'way. The man jus' fold up an' crumple 'pon the ground. Him life gone, tek 'way by dat dyam bitch. Me look 'pon Deacon remains an' could see me nex' so me haffe start t'ink quick.

"Ole Hige, in the meanwhile, ah lick her lips an' you could ah see the blood ah travel her body, through the veins an' t'ing. She look 'pon me an' mek a dreadful screaming noise. As she go fe jump 'pon me, me tek me bottle ah Bay Rum an' Kananga Water an' wet up the bitch. Her flesh start smoke an' sizzle an' she jus' ah scream an' ah pitch from one side to the other. The dyam dawg drop ah ground an' ah roll inna the dutty fe rub off the sint'ing. Two twos, she raise up an' ah fly 'round me head fe try an' suck out me life. Me pick up one piece ah stick you see an' start batter the devil anytime she come nex' to me. Me did give her one bitch lick an' she start wail. She fly an' go 'round an' go 'round 'til she ah fly straight at me. Me duck an' pop the bitch shoulder with the stick.

"Me tek foot then an' when me look back, me see Ole Hige ah laugh an' ah put back on her skin."

PickneyDaddy shook his head as his tale came to an end. "You evah see Ole Hige again?" Ella asked.

"Oh no," PickneyDaddy said, shaking his head. "Me know dat brute nah spare me nex' time."

"Me did see Ole Miller the other night an' no-one nah believe we."

"Cho'," PickneyDaddy kissed his teeth. "Unuh pickney can tell worser story than me..." he smiled, heading off home.

NINE
Deliverance

Jim was up early in the morning, cursing loudly as he rummaged through a cardboard box in the front room.

"Is wha' you ah do so?" Mom Butler called from the bedroom. She was tired after all the events of the past few days and had decided to have a lie-in, telling the children to take the day off school. But it was as if her husband hadn't heard her. He continued cursing and rummaging. Mom Butler heard a sudden crash from the kitchen.

"Dyam an' blast to hell," she mumbled, climbing out of bed and storming through the door.

"Is wha' you ah do?" she asked again, with her hands on her hips. Jim stopped rummaging and looked up at her. His face still bore the tiredness and fatigue of the previous nights, but apart from that he was in good spirits.

"Hush nuh, woman, you nuh see me ah do somet'ing important? When man have trouble, woman take it make laugh."

Mom Butler drew breath, and fired back another proverb,

"when trouble tek man, pickney boot fit him. Jim," she said calmly, "if yuh nah tell me wha' ah gwan, ah going send fe the Doctor ah Belview."

Jim simply chuckled as he pulled out a sheet of blue paper.

"See it yah!" he announced joyfully, picking himself up and planting a sloppy kiss on Mom Butler's cheek, to her surprise.

"Me have it!" Jim crowed, holding the blue paper in the air and dancing around.

"Stop!" Mom Butler shouted, halting Jim in his tracks. She was puzzled by his behaviour and wanted to know what all the excitement was about. She tugged the sheet of paper from his hand and unravelled it, focusing on the handwritten words before her.

"Y'see," Jim said, grinning broadly. "Dis piece ah paper ah the agreement."

"You ah idiot?" Mom Butler asked pointedly. "Dis ah the lease fe the land the Johnson dem have, dat's all."

Jim nodded, "yes, but is not a lease, is jus' ah agreement. Is not bound by law." Jim's eyes sparkled menacingly as a broad smile washed his face.

"Is wha' you ah seh?" Mom Butler asked as she lowered herself into a chair.

"Bwoy," Jim started, rubbing the stubble on his chin casually. "Dem haffe go." He'd been hoping that he'd find this sheet of paper. If the Johnsons wanted to take him to court, this agreement would never stand up and after what he'd learned about their role in his daughter's illness, he wanted them off the land. He was going to get rid of them once and for all.

"Wha' you ah go do?" she shouted as Jim disappeared into the bedroom.

"Wha' ah gwan, Mom?" Ella yawned, appearing at the kitchen door.

146

"Me nuh know wha' ah gwan, me dear. Yuh daddy up to somet'ing strange. Him forget that cock can't beat cock inna cock own yard." Mom Butler went to the bedroom after her husband. Bill came in asking, "wha's all the noise about?" His sister shrugged.

"Me ah go ketch some janga, you ah come?" he told Ella.

"Inna dat deh cold water?" Ella queried wrapping her arms around her.

"Come on, gal, you need some fresh air," Bill said persuasively.

"A'right," Ella gave in, "mek me jus' wash an' brush up me hair."

Mom Butler had found Jim sitting in the bedroom pulling on a pair of boots riddled with holes.

"You nah dash 'way dem dutty sint'ing dem. Dem ah stink up the whole place," she said, before she pegged her nose with her fingers as if to block out some nasty smell.

"Why you nuh mind yuh own business?" Jim responded light-heartedly as he struggled to push his feet down into the boots.

"Nuh tell me so," Mom Butler shouted playfully, attempting to hit Jim across the head. But Jim was too quick. He ducked, evading the back sweep as he scrambled to his feet and stood his ground.

"Me busy yah, me nuh have no time fe ramp," he said, trying to be serious as he straightened the creases in his trousers.

"It look like you ah dress off fe go meet the Queen," Mom Butler remarked. Jim smiled and for a moment he lost himself in nostalgic thoughts. He smiled again, this time with a huge grin lighting up his face.

"Is wha' sweet you so," Mom Butler chuckled, seeing her

147

husband in such good spirits.

"Not'n," Jim replied secretively.

"You mussi have one woman ah street then...you fe 'member that two dog fe one bone, two woman fe one house, nevah agree long," his wife teased.

Jim had decided that it was about time the long-standing bad feeling between himself and his spouse should be aired and thrown out into the open once and for all. It had been too long since they had sat down and really talked, neither of them wishing to admit that they had a problem in their marriage or to deal with the matter.

"Is time we ah reason, Grace," he said seriously. Mom Butler looked at Jim in a sort of confused way.

"Deal with wha'?" she said, kissing her teeth. Jim's innocent suggestion seemed to fire up something in Mom Butler's mind. Something she didn't want to bring up, but something that had been on her mind every day. It was something they still hadn't sorted out. "We nuh have not'n fe chat 'bout. You done all yuh chatting when you mek Little Jakie go to him casket."

"Bwoy," Jim said in resignation, "you still deh 'pon dat t'ing." He slumped back on the bed and folded his body up in a ball as if to withdraw from the whole situation. Mom Butler watched her husband and felt sympathy for him. She wanted, so badly, to embrace him, but she was unable to let down the uncompromising brick wall which seemed destined to force them apart.

"How you can be so bitter after all dis time? You nuh feel seh me have to deal with the bwoy death too? All me see every day is the poor bwoy ah fall over the gully. Me feel it too. Ah jus' bad luck."

For a long tense moment there was silence, then Mom Butler had something to say.

148

"Jim," she began, "you feel me can forget so easy? Is me son. If you nevah so stupid the bwoy would ah here now. Instead you gone ah rum shop ah drink out yuh life an' mek the bwoy run to him death. Bad luck worse than obeah..." Mom Butler stopped her tears in time.

"Is me son too," Jim said soberly as his head dropped into his hands. "How you t'ink me feel?"

"Me nuh waan know," Mom Butler said sharply, turning back to confront him. "Monkey should know whe' him going put his tail before him order trousers. You know me nuh even know if me can trust you again. Me nuh even know if me can love you like before."

The room suddenly went silent as both of them stared at each other with glistening eyes.

"All Bill and Ella..." Mom Butler continued.

Jim looked up and his face dropped even further. He knew what was about to come and he didn't want to hear it.

"The poor bwoy don't know if him coming or going. All you ah do the bwoy is cuss an' beat him. But Ella, you show her all the love and it show so plain dat she is yuh favourite. You can't gwan so, dem will start hate each other if you carry on so."

Mom Butler had said her piece and Jim felt well chastised. He sulked a little.

"It nuh go so," he said, trying to defend himself and the difficult situation with his son.

"No?" Mom Butler queried, a line appeared on her face and seemed to dissect her features.

"Grace," he said, working hard to ensure the right words came out, "you know the bwoy nuh like me too tough an' him feel seh him is a big man."

"Him is a bwoy, an' dat's all him is," Mom Butler summed

up. "Anyway, him will grow up fe hate you if you nuh mek a effort to sort yuh problems out."

"Me waan fe sort t'ings out between us," Jim admitted to Mom. Slowly he picked himself off of the bed. "Give me a kiss nuh," he said playfully.

"No, Jim," Mom Butler drew away. "Me have too much t'inking fe do 'bout us, an' me nuh ready fe gwan like happy families."

Jim nodded reluctantly as he forced his arm into the sleeve of a jacket. "Me soon come," he said. He attempted to kiss his wife again but failed. As he stepped out of their bedroom he only narrowly avoided bashing into Ella and Bill, who were about to go down to the river.

"Morning son," Jim said, with a bright, wide smile.

"Morning," said Bill in reply, smiling as his father rushed out of the house. Moments later, Bill and Ella also left the house.

"You did ah dream last night?" Bill asked Ella as he set a brisk pace away from the house.

"Yeah, me dream Ole Miller again."

Bill shivered, but said nothing. That was one dream he didn't want to hear about.

They walked down to the bend in the road where Ole Miller's house stood. They approached it in silence. Ella stopped in front of the gate. Again, it was open, this time wider than before. She looked at her brother, who shook his head negatively. There was no time and anyway they had no right. But this time Ella's mind was made up. Her curiosity needed to be quenched or she would never be content.

"El!" Bill called, but it was too late, his sister was already through the gate and inside Ole Miller's compound. He had no choice but to go with her.

"El," he called out again in a hushed voice.

But Ella was deaf to his appeals. She had noticed that the front door stood slightly ajar—just like in her dream—and she tiptoed up to it, pushing it even wider open onto a large hallway, which seemed strangely cleaner than she had imagined. There was not a cobweb in sight and everything seemed to have been maintained. Now she was inside, Ella became frightened. What was she doing here? What did she hope to achieve. Supposing Ole Miller suddenly showed up, what was she going to say. How was she going to explain trespassing on his property. She held her breath for a moment and listened intently. The only thing she could hear was the dull thud of her own heart pumping. She was about to turn to go, when suddenly she felt a hand on her shoulder and she let out a shriek.

But it was only Bill.

"Me... me nearly die ah fright," she whispered. "You nearly turn me into duppy, Bill."

"El, wha' you want in yah?"

"Me nuh know," El confessed.

"Monkey should know whe' him gwine put him tail before him order trousers, y'know?" Bill echoed one of his mother's favourite proverbs.

Suddenly from somewhere in the house a loud voice echoed: "AH WHO DAT?"

Ella and Bill looked at each other with terror in their eyes. They didn't need to be asked again. Both quickly turned and ran back out of the house. Already they could hear footsteps coming after them.

"Him ah come fe get we!"

As Ella reached the gate, the thought that she was safe crossed her mind, but in the same instant, she heard her

151

brother Bill cry out in pain, as he lost his balance and fell to the dusty ground of Ole Miller's front yard.

As Ella turned to assist her brother she saw the figure of Ole Miller running towards Bill.

"We come fe get we ball!" Ella cried out , half in- and half outside the gate, as Ole Miller stood over her brother. Fear was making her mind tick fast. "We lost we ball an' we can't find it," she continued. Still Ole Miller didn't move, but stood over Bill as if considering what to do. Bill, reeled around on the ground in pain, holding his ankle.

"What yuh was doing in 'ere? You pickney too dyam nosy. You hurt yuh foot?" Ole Miller asked him.

"Y…y….y…yeah," Bill stuttered, looking up at the scruffily dressed man standing above him, his eyes sunk deep into his head, his hair speckled with grey and the worry lines of many years spread across his forehead.

"Me know unuh pickney from over so," he nodded in the direction of their house. "You is Jim Butler's son."

"You is Ole Miller?" Ella asked, still prepared to run if necessary.

This was the same man she'd seen in church.

"Ole Miller? Oh, you mean Richard Miller. No, me name Collins, Detective Collins. Kingston Police Force." He pulled a wallet out of the pocket of his shabby raincoat and flashed his I.D.

"Police?" Ella blurted.

"From Kingston?" her brother added.

Collins nodded. Ella and Bill's eyes widened as Collins explained that Ole Miller was dead. He had been dead for a long time before the police found him, calling on the house during their routine inquiries a couple of days before. Collins was only here now to check out the house and to satisfy himself of the fact that Mr Miller had had nothing to do with the murders.

"Me can't believe it! Ole Miller, dead?"

"Its true," said Detective Collins, "and don't go snooping around in strange places. Yuh shouldn't even be 'ere. Yuh should go and do your chores." With that he turned and disappeared back into the house.

"Dat man too rude," said Bill, annoyed at being ordered around by a policeman who was no better than a school bully.

"He's only doing his job."

As Bill and Ella watched him go they noticed a trail of people heading towards them. Syd Johnson headed the group followed by Kai, Ivan and Marian Johnson.

"Look like trouble," said Bill, and they hurried home.

Jim was back, standing on the verandah.

"Dada!" Ella cried out, "the Johnsons dem ah come."

Jim Butler pushed the front door open and hauled his children in. "Me know," he said soberly, closing the door firmly behind him.

"Wha' ah gwan?" Bill asked, panting and out of breath.

"Me decide fe get rough with dem ignorant people. Me tell dem fe lef' me place by nex' week," Jim announced.

"You ah joke?" said Bill.

"Me nah joke," Jim replied. "Look 'pon dis." Jim showed his son a copy of the notice to quit. Bill shook his head.

"You can't do dis."

"Who tell you so?"

"Dada, you can't mek dem homeless," Bill pleaded.

"Mek me explain somet'ing to you, pickney, 'cause it coming like you nuh understand not'n. You mussi did forget the other day when Ella sick. Well me nah forget dat an' you know why, 'cause dat dyam Johnson woman set somet'ing

153

'pon my child."

Bill and Ella listened in silence. The Johnsons were at the house now.

"But dem nuh have nowhere fe go…"

Suddenly, the door rattled under a barrage of fists. "Come out, Butler," a voice shouted. "Come out, we waan reason with you."

It was Mom Butler who made the first move, coming out of the kitchen where she had been waiting, and leaning against the half-open front door.

"You lose somet'ing?" she asked, staring Marian Johnson in the face. Marian's face glowed with menace as her forehead creased.

"Dis ah foolishness," Marian rolled the eviction notice into a ball and threw it on the verandah, just as Jim Butler appeared.

"Dat ah nuh not'n," he said. "Me have a copy in a safe place."

"You can't enforce dat deh notice without bringing me to court."

"You nevah read the sint'ing properly. Me nuh haffe go ah no court."

"Who tell you so?" Kai interjected. "We have rights."

Jim looked grudgingly at Ivan and kissed his teeth. "Mek me tell unuh somet'ing," he began, "unuh nuh have no rights more than me 'llow unuh fe live 'pon the land. And dat's all. You see dis agreement? Read it. It seh, '…by the agreement of Jim Butler, Mr and Mrs Johnson will be permitted to live on the premises named above, until reasonable notice is given, thus giving vacant possession to Jim Butler…' Dat ah the original agreement from all twelve years since. So tek yuh raas off me doorstep an' start pack yuh t'ings."

Syd and his two uncles both stood with their fists clenched.

Marian Johnson threw herself at the mercy of her half-sister. "How you can throw out me an' me pickney dem 'pon street? You nuh have no heart?"

Where would they go? She began weeping.

"Save yuh tears," Jim said coldly, keeping a wary eye on Ivan and Kai. "You see, me is not a cold-hearted man but fe wha' you do, me can't forget."

"So is wha' you ah try seh?" Marian wiped at her eyes.

"Me nah try seh not'n," Jim responded sharply. "Wha' me ah seh is you set somet'ing fe me an' me family. Nuh bother gwan like you nuh know wha' me ah talk 'bout. You set obeah fe we."

Marian's expression told another story. She still claimed she didn't know what Jim was talking about. She tried to reason.

"Me nah change me mind, y'know," he said.

"How you can seh we try fe obeah you, Butler? Ah nuh a dyam lie you ah tell 'pon we?" Kai said angrily. "We nuh trouble dem sint'ing deh," he continued.

"Cho'," Jim murmured. "Jus' come off me land an' go ah yuh yard."

"You can't fling we out so, please," Marian begged, but Jim was in no mood to bargain.

"Ah so you feel? Me want you outta me place."

"You know how much pickney me have?"

"Cho', you ah joke," Jim jibed. "You have no chance with me again."

The words seemed final. Marian saw the determined look in his eyes. There was no way he was going to change his mind.

"Come," Marian said as she turned to leave.

Then Ivan spoke, his forehead creased, his mood darkened. "You can't jus' lef' so. We nuh have nowhere fe go if we lef' the yard."

"Come, we nah beg smaddy fe not'n."

Reluctantly, dejectedly, the Johnsons turned one by one and headed back to their home.

"Jim," Mom Butler began, "maybe we should reconsider…" Mom Butler's feeling of guilt was showing through. But Jim was unmoveable, and it made no difference that Marian Johnson was his wife's half-sister.

"But dem nuh have nowhere fe go. Imagine," Mom Butler paused, pondering her thoughts, "you did kick out 'pon road with yuh family, with nowhere fe go, wha' you would ah do?"

"Dem can go an' find one coconut tree fe live under," Jim said dismissively.

"Me serious, Jim."

"But, Grace, dem did try fe kill Ella. Dat nuh mean not'n to you?"

"But we don't know dat fe certain. Nah true?"

Jim looked across at his wife. He couldn't believe what she was saying. She who had been so eager to turn to an obeah worker to heal her daughter. "You mean to tell me seh dat you ah tek side against me fe the Johnson dem? You t'ink me ah use Ella's sickness fe get dem offa the land? Dat ah stupidness an' you know it."

"Me nah tek sides, but me not sure dat dem set somet'ing fe Ella."

"Bwoy," Jim began, scratching his hair, "after all the t'ings dat happen to yuh family, you still defending Marian. Cho', you an' her ah the same…"

Jim couldn't have imagined what the impact of his words would be. Nobody had ever said that before, but in some ways she was like Marian and why not? They were sisters, after all. Before tears began to fall, Mom Butler decided to leave the conversation. She went into her bedroom, where she tried to

156

regain her composure. That night she would think long and hard about her mother, her father and her half-sister. And again and again she would come to the conclusion that blood was thicker than water.

The old man studied the faces of his guests with a curious look of recognition. Their bushy, unkempt appearance and their dark complexions reminded him of someone who had come to see him only a few weeks earlier.

The two men shifted uneasily on their chairs, both sweating profusely. They wanted to do their business and go, as soon as possible.

The walls of the small shack were bare and built with a mix of the same earth as that which lay under the soles of their workman boots. The flicker of a flame down in the far left corner was the only illumination, and it made the man sitting opposite them seem even more sinister.

"Is this what you really want?" the cool, kindly voice asked, almost unconcerned.

"Yes," the two men answered together without hesitation. They had argued with Marian enough. She wanted to rely on prayer. They had decided to put their trust somewhere else. This was something they should have done a long time ago. They wanted the life of Jim Butler and nothing less.

They handed him the content of their crocus bag.

The man nodded. "You can go now. I will take care of everyt'ing."

TEN
Revelations

Barnabas Collins stretched out one of his legs. The pins and needles that had slowly deadened one leg were now creeping up the other as he crouched down low amidst the dense shrubbery. It was only the second time he'd been to this part of the parish and he was beginning to feel very uneasy. It was unnaturally quiet and even a sceptic like himself felt very uncomfortable. Maybe there was some truth to the stories shrouding the small village's existence.

He shrugged off his uneasiness as he surveyed the surroundings. He was hiding in a ring of high thick bushes that encircled a small clearing. There was a large dusty yard in front with a short clothes line stretching between two wooden posts and a couple of clothes baskets nearby, but apart from that the yard was clear. Towards the back of the clearing was a small wooden shack. Obviously the obeah man's house.

Stylehut. Obeah. The two words were synonymous. If Ivan and Kai had come to this remote village then they had plans to use obeah to get back at the Butlers. He was well aware of the

158

rivalry between the two families, following the incident he'd witnessed outside the Johnson house when Jim had been released from prison. There was some really bad blood between them. But that wasn't the reason behind him following the two brothers here. He'd driven up to the Johnson house to ask Marian some more questions about her late husband. But when he'd parked his car he'd noticed the two brothers leaving the house, one of them carefully concealing a small sack under his coat. The detective's curiosity had got the better of him and he'd quickly jumped out of his vehicle to follow at a discreet distance.

The bushes to his left moved and Collins jumped. He looked closer and noticed a large black cat looking up at him. Where are dem dyam men? he thought to himself as he shooed the cat away. He could just see the clearing through the bushes and beyond it the small wooden shack that the two brothers had disappeared into.

Suddenly there was a movement from the side of the shack and a small yard dog appeared, sniffing the ground as if scavenging for food. At the same time, the small door that led into the shack opened and Ivan and Kai Johnson appeared, looking pleased with themselves.

Collins watched the men leave and was about to follow them when he heard a low growling noise nearby. The yard dog must have picked up the scent of the cat and found its way over to his hiding place. It was now trying to root him out of the bushes. If he didn't move soon, the dog would be upon him and he'd lose the two men. He looked back towards the Johnsons, but they hadn't noticed and were walking briskly away.

With a loud bark of triumph the dog broke suddenly through the bush and latched itself onto the detective's leg.

"What the hell...?" He frantically tried to shake the dog off but it had fastened itself to his trouser leg.

"If you cyan come off by yuhself, me will mek you come off." Collins grappled for something, anything that he could use to free himself. His hand settled on a small round pebble and he threw it with force. But the dog saw him raise his arm and went down on its haunches. The stone sailed over its head.

Collins felt around again. If he didn't get away from this blasted dog he'd surely lose the Johnson brothers or, worse still, his leg. He saw what looked like a piece of an old walking stick and quickly reached for it. The dog was busying itself by pulling hard on his now ripped trouser leg, viciously shaking its head from side to side and snarling manically. Collins slowly brought the stick up and hit the dog hard on its back. It immediately let go and backed off, whimpering pitifully.

Detective Collins held the stick up threateningly as he scrambled to his feet, but the dog was nursing its injuries and had no intention of attacking again.

"Now where dem men go?" said Collins to himself. He quickly left the bush and was soon on the narrow path that led away from the clearing.

The red soil was compact and hard under the policeman's feet and as he hurried to catch up with his prey he was immediately reminded of the three murdered victims of the Swinger. Both of the adult victims had the same red soil under their shoes and Bubsy, who had been barefoot when he'd taken his last breath, had had distinctly red dust on the bottom of his feet. He hadn't seen this rich russet red soil anywhere else on the island and now here it was in Stylehut. He remembered the press cutting about two Stylehut hangings a few years back. Everything seemed to lead back to this village. Each of the victims had obviously been here during the last few hours of their lives. But why? It could only be for one thing...

As Collins broke through onto the main path that led back towards Duppy Bridge, Ivan and Kai were nowhere to be seen. They surely couldn't have gotten very far. Maybe they'd heard the commotion that that dumb yard dog had caused and decided to get out of the area, and fast. Dyam and blast!

He quickly ran up the path, taking the odd moment to check the bushes as he went. If the Johnson brothers were hiding in there, they weren't going to take this policeman by surprise.

Suddenly, a blood-curdling scream filled the night air. Collins froze. "A wha' the raas..?" It had come from the direction of Duppy Bridge.

The policeman stepped up his pace, rushing onwards with only the moonlight to guide him. Maybe the brothers had had some disagreement and a fight had ensued; maybe in the darkness one of them had fallen down the gully; but, maybe, the Swinger had struck again...

And with that thought preying on his mind, Collins came into the clearing that was Duppy Bridge. Only when he'd stopped did he realize how quiet it was and only then when he looked up did he notice the horrifying sight before his eyes. Hanging from the only tree in this part of Stylehut were two bodies.

Ivan's body was still twitching.

Collins ran up to him, grabbing him by the legs and frantically trying to lift his body higher to ease the pressure around his neck. His attempt was in vain, however; Ivan soon joined his brother in the afterworld.

The Swinger had struck again and Ivan and Kai Johnson had been its latest victims. And one question came back to the detective's mind. A question that had plagued him since the first of these murders. How the hell had the Swinger been able to string up his victims all by himself? And, leading on from that, how had he managed to kill them so quickly?

Detective Collins looked around as if expecting the Swinger to show himself. Being a policeman didn't mean you were superhuman and inside his mind was in turmoil. These latest events had introduced a new line of enquiry. The red soil around Duppy Bridge and Stylehut was the one significant factor in all of these murders. And, with the possible exception of Bubsy, all of the murdered people could have had a reason to visit the obeah man here. Well, he'd just have to bring this obeah man into the station for questioning.

Ella was up at the Swinging Tree with Bill. At last, she felt ready to talk about her first hand experience of obeah and her brother wanted to know all the details.

"So how yuh did feel, El? asked Bill as he sat with his back against one of the coconut trees. He was holding a long, thin stick and was using it to dig a hole in the soil nearby.

Ella looked at her brother and tried to remember how she had felt. Since recovering from her mysterious illness she hadn't really thought about it, preferring to get on with her life. Now she focused her mind back to the day of the race. She remembered the nightmares she had had the night before and recounted them to Bill in as much detail as she could remember.

"Me not sure if dem was part ah the obeah," said Ella, "but dem did really frighten me."

"Dem was all part of the same t'ing," Bill said with conviction. He'd heard enough stories to feel sure that the dreams his sister had suffered were only the beginning of the curse that had been inflicted upon her.

"Then, after the race, me jus' start to feel really bad: some horrible cramps and the pain…" Ella's face screwed up as she recalled the sensation. Bill stopped digging and looked up at her sympathetically. "But then after dat I can't remember much."

The two fell silent after that, Ella swinging on her tree, Bill resuming his digging.

"Me was really worried," Bill said after a while. "Me did t'ink say you were goin' fe dead."

"Like Bubsy?" said a third voice.

Bill and Ella started.

"Who's dat?" asked Bill, standing up and brandishing the stick as a weapon.

The bushes around the clearing rustled and Jacqueline, the late Bubsy's girlfriend, appeared. Her eyes were red and puffy and tears streamed down her cheeks.

Bill and Ella visibly relaxed.

"Is only me," she said rubbing her eyes, "me jus' come from your house an yuh mother say yuh is up here."

"Buy wha' you doing out by yuhself?" asked Ella as she jumped off the swing. Then she saw how upset her friend was. "Wha' wrong?"

"It's Bubsy…" the girl began and, before she could continue, she broke down, sobbing shamelessly.

It took some time to calm Jacqueline down enough for her to explain what was upsetting her. And although Bill and Ella had no idea what was troubling the girl, one thing was certain. Their friend was very scared.

"Me t'ink say me is going to get kill next," said Jacqueline once she'd regained her composure. She went and sat down under a coconut tree.

Bill and Ella exchanged incredulous looks before following

her over.

"So wha mek you t'ink dis?" asked Ella.

"Me didn't tell anyone 'bout dis, so you haffe swear not to say anything," she waited for their confirmation.

They nodded.

"Well, when Bubsy disappear down ah Cane an' Tobacco Farm, him didn't really disappear."

"Wha' you mean?" asked Bill sharply.

"He didn't disappear, 'cause I know where he did ah go really." Jacqueline looked down sheepishly.

"So where he dida go?"

"He went to see one obeah man down ah Stylehut."

Bill stepped back shocked. Bubsy had gone to visit an obeah man by himself! But why would he need to? He looked back at Jacqueline who had started to cry again.

"Him did say dat he needed to get back at some bully at school," she continued between sobs, "he dida want me fe go with him, but I was scared."

Ella was standing with her mouth open. She couldn't believe what she was hearing. What was the matter with everyone? Why did they all go running to the obeah man when they had a problem? Still, she was mesmerized by the tale and urged Jacqueline on. "So wha' happen then?"

"Me went with him in the end. He tell me say its alright and so I went with him. I too fool fool," she said, almost to herself. "When we reach Duppy Bridge I start to get frighten again, so me tell Bubsy that I will wait for him there. But when him gone me did feel too scared to wait around there, so me lef' and went to school." The girl wiped her arm across her eyes. "Dat was the last time me see him..."

Bill went and sat next to Jacqueline. "So why you so upset now?"

The girl looked up into Bill's eyes. "Because when you use obeah for badness, it come back to get you. Dat's what my mamma always tell me, dat's what happen to Bubsy and because I was with him it's coming fe me."

Bill looked at Ella briefly before replying. "Dat's only true if yuh is the one dat tek out the obeah," he said with authority. "You didn't go with him to see the man, so yuh is alright."

Jacqueline turned to Ella, as if in need of further confirmation. Ella nodded. "Is true. My dada always tell me so."

The distraught teenager seemed to relax at this: it was the first time in a long while that she had felt at ease. "So yuh mean me been worrying 'bout nothing?"

"Dat's right. Yuh didn't see no obeah man and yuh didn't use obeah for no badness, so yuh have no worries. But I tell you one thing," said Bill, as if in sudden realisation of a fact that should have been obvious before now, "it come like the Swinger don't like people using obeah for badness either."

ELEVEN
Duppy Conqueror

The four walls of the interrogation room were blank and grey, offering no form of distraction to those unlucky enough to be inside. Rooms like this were very familiar to Detective Collins, he had spent hours in them when working on a case, questioning suspects, getting confessions out of the guilty. He was ready for a confession today.

He looked at the old man sitting on the other side of the table. He was a slim man, whose silver-grey locks suggested that he had seen many years. He seemed unphased by his surroundings and was calmly returning the policeman's stare. This wasn't going to be easy, thought Collins.

Darcus Lindo was a man of power in his small community. As the most frequently used obeah man in Stylehut, he had become the well respected, unofficial head of the village. Thus, when the policemen raided his small hut, the villagers nearby had reacted with surprising speed. As Collins and two arresting officers had emerged from Lindo's home, members of the small community had already lined the main path leading

166

to Duppy Bridge where the police car was parked. The people hadn't reacted with any violence or threats, they'd merely stood, silently watching, some muttering quiet chants, all staring with questioning, hostile eyes.

Collins had felt very unnerved then, but now, in the familiar surroundings of the police station, he felt completely in control.

Lindo took out his pipe: a long wooden stem with a bowl carved from coconut.

"Yuh cyaan smoke in 'ere," said Collins quickly.

Lindo put the pipe on the table without complaint.

"So, Darcus, where were you on the day Robert Johnson was killed?"

"Mr Lindo."

"Sorry?"

"Yuh mus' call me by name: Mr Lindo." He spoke the words without feeling, as if detached from the situation.

"Okay, *Mr Lindo*, where were you?"

Lindo carefully picked up his pipe again, knocking the bowl on the table to clean out the old weed. "Where were *you*, detective?"

Collins slammed his fist down on the table. They'd only just begun the session and already this pathetic little obeah man was irritating him. Why couldn't he just answer the question? "Look, Mr Obeah man, I don't t'ink you understand what's going on 'ere. Five people have been killed an' so far me don't have no killer."

The obeah man was silent and, ignoring the policeman's earlier statement about smoking, took out a small pouch of weed and started to load up his pipe.

"NO SMOKING!!" Collins shouted.

"You mus' keep calm. Anger ah boil up yuh inside, me cyan see it. Or wha', you waan heart attack?" Lindo placed the weed

167

on the table in front of him and leant back in his chair. He scratched his chin absentmindedly, a gesture he repeated over and over again, an unconscious habit. "Me was at home."

"You have anyone dat can back you up?"

"No," Lindo paused. "But tell me, Detective Collins, you evah hear 'bout the killer whose spirit killed when his body slept? Do you know where your spirit was dat day?"

Detective Collins ignored the question and stood up, walking around the table until he was standing right behind his interviewee. Suddenly, he grabbed the obeah man, wrapping his arm tightly around his neck, hauling the old man out of his chair. "You ready fe answer my questions now, huh?"

Lindo gripped the detective's arm in an attempt to free himself, but without success. He struggled for a few seconds more then nodded slightly to indicate his acquiescence. Collins slowly released him. Now, maybe, he could get somewhere with this man.

The detective took a sheet of paper out of his jacket pocket. It was a list of all the murdered victims. "Did all the people dem come to you fe obeah?"

The old man looked at the short list and nodded again. Yes, thought Collins, I have the link now. He walked around the room slowly, deliberately.

"How you did string dem up?"

Darcus Lindo's light brown eyes were amazingly bright for someone of his advanced years, looking more like the eyes of a younger man. Collins found it hard to hold his gaze.

"Dem did choose their own path..." said the old man plainly.

"Wha' you mean?"

"Jus' wha' me seh. If you play with fire, you will always get burnt."

"So you did have a reason to kill dem?" said Collins. He had his man and was closing in for the kill.

"Me nevah seh dat," said Lindo, relaxing back into his seat again and stroking his chin contemplatively. "Dem didn't understand wha' dem ah deal wid. If you use obeah for badness, it will come back fe you. Yuh mudda nevah tell you dat, Detective?"

"So yuh tryin' to tell me dat is obeah kill dem?"

"Dem kill demself," replied Lindo. "As will you," he added so quietly it was almost inaudible. Almost but not quite.

"Wha' you ah seh?"

But the obeah man had closed his eyes and was chanting under his breath.

Let him stay there and chant, thought the policeman. He isn't going anywhere until I have a confession, so he might as well make himself comfortable. Maybe I should string up a couple of chicken feet and a cow's heart to make him really feel at home. He smiled to himself.

The chanting grew louder and suddenly Detective Collins started to feel weak. The interrogation room swirled around him: the grey of the walls merging with the grey of the ceiling until he was unsure of whether he was standing or lying. He allowed himself to fall into the chair opposite the obeah man. Darcus Lindo was manipulating something in the palm of his hand, pulling at it and rubbing the object as he chanted.

Collins' vision began to blur and somewhere deep within himself he could hear the voice of reason screaming for an explanation. He vaguely saw Lindo get up and walk over to him. He placed the object he carried on the table, just out of the policeman's reach. Collins recognized his own watch. He mus' have got hold of it when I tried to choke him, he thought wildly.

Lindo was standing over him now. Collins tried to lift his arm to push him away, but he seemed to have no control over his body. He felt completely numb from the neck down and he was slowly losing consciousness.

The very last thing he saw was the obeah man making strange signs in the air above his head. Then he blacked out.

At the Butler house Jim, Mom, Bill and Ella were waiting patiently for the arrival of Marian Johnson. Everyone in the parish had heard about the tragic death of her two brothers and feelings were running high.

Mom Butler had immediately sent Bill down to Marian's house to ask her to come up, saying that they needed to talk. They had to put the feud behind them and see if they could come to some sort of arrangement over the land. The most important thing now was that they were family and family should stick together. She knew that Jim didn't agree, especially since he now knew that Jakie's death was tied in with the same obeah that had affected Ella. But desperate people did desperate things and Marian had got her payback, thrice over. She only hoped that Jim would come round.

There was a knock at the door and Ella jumped out of her armchair to answer it. A stern look from her mother forced her back to her seat.

"Bill, answer the door," Mom Butler said, "and, Jim, please jus' keep calm."

Jim kissed his teeth.

Seconds later Marian Johnson and her son Syd walked into the room. She seemed smaller somehow, as if all the traumas of the last weeks had finally caught up with her and were

170

pounding her into the ground. Her expression was pensive and her grief showed clearly on her face. Sid was a shadow of his former self, refusing to look at anything but the ground. Despite everything that he had done, Ella felt a little sorry for him.

"Marian, me is so sorry…" began Mom Butler.

Marian shook her head, "No, Grace, me is the one who should be saying sorry. There's no excuse for what Robert did do to Ella. Me did try to stop Ivan and Kai from going to the obeah man again, but dem is too ignorant. Me did tell dem that not'n good would come of it, now look wha' 'appen…"

Ella looked over at her half-aunty shyly.

Mom Butler motioned to them to sit down. They all sat in silence while they took in what Marian had just said.

"Listen," said Mom Butler breaking the silence, "the reason me call you here was to sort out our problems once and for all."

Marian nodded, but remained silent.

"Some bad t'ings did happen between our mothers, but we haffe let go of the past. The more I t'ink 'bout it, the more I want us to put it behind us. My little Jakie is dead and I almost lose my Ella, all because of dis feud. Me tired now, me want it fe end." Mom Butler looked at Jim, but he deliberately chose not to return her stare.

"So how yuh feel 'bout dis, Jim?" asked Marian, turning to her brother-in-law. If his behaviour up to now was anything to go by then he wouldn't agree to a truce. She thought about her little house, about the fact that she could soon be leaving it forever, about where she would go if Jim insisted that she left. Everything she knew and loved could soon be taken cruelly away from her.

All eyes turned to Jim.

Mom Butler silently prayed that her husband would finally

see how pointless it was to throw the Johnsons off their land. They'd had a long discussion about it when the news had first reached them about Ivan and Kai. And when they'd discovered the location of the bodies, Jim had blown a fuse, "Dem Johnson man mussi gone' back up there fe obeah again. Who it was going to be nex'? Me? Bill? You, Mom? No dem Johnsons is one an' the same an the sooner they come off my land the bettah."

Once the children had gone off to school, the couple had argued long and hard, moving away from discussing the Johnsons and, inevitably, as the majority of their arguments did, onto the death of Jakie. They'd shouted, screamed, blamed one another again and then, after all the pain and guilt and heartache had been exposed, a calm had fallen on the room.

"I feel as though it's my han' dat kill Jakie," Jim had said quietly.

Mom Butler had sighed, "me tired, Jim. I don't wan' to argue wid you any more. Jakie's gone now and not'n will bring him back. You haffe stop dat drinking and get on with yuh life. Yuh still have two pickney lef'."

Jim had looked at his wife and nodded.

Now as everyone sat waiting for his response to Marian's question, Jim remembered the way Mom Butler had smiled and squeezed his arm when he'd agreed to try to change. Maybe there was still a chance for them to be a family, despite the death of their child. He looked around the room. At Marian and Syd, widowed, fatherless. Then at Ella, who'd come so close to death herself only days earlier; at his son, Bill, who he felt he didn't really know, and then, lastly, at Mom Butler. Whatever he said now would determine the way his life would go on.

He took a deep breath, "it's jus' like Grace say, we haffe sort dis out. We can talk about the land, but this feud mus' come to an end."

A loud scream sounded from the police interrogation room.

"Ah wha' the blouse an' skirt?" asked one of the duty officers, a young timid-looking man who normally tried to avoid any action.

"Me nuh know," said his older colleague, "but me gwine find out."

He grabbed a bunch of keys from under the front desk and ran up the short hallway that led to the cells and the interrogation room. The younger man followed at a short distance.

When they reached the door all they could hear was the sound of a scuffle from inside. The older, more experienced policeman unhooked his gun from its holster and mouthed the words, *AFTER THREE*, to the second man who, reluctantly, nodded agreement. They counted together and slammed open the door.

The scene that greeted them was shocking.

The small table had been turned on its side and the two chairs lay broken. But it was the sight from the far corner of the room that was the most horrifying.

Detective Collins was on the floor on all fours, his tongue hanging out of his open mouth, whilst Darcus Lindo, the obeah man, sat calmly astride him like a jockey.

The two policeman exchanged a puzzled stare before the older man spurred himself into action. "DETECTIVE COLLINS!" he shouted. " Stop wha' yuh ah do and move away from the man."

But the detective seemed not to hear or was so determined to carry the obeah man on his back that he simply wouldn't hear.

The two men rushed over to their superior officer and when the younger officer looked into Barnabas Collins' face he stepped back in horror. His face was completely vacant, devoid of any emotion.

"Winston, me need yuh help!" said the older officer who was still trying to pull Lindo off the detective's back.

Winston pulled himself together and gripped the obeah man in a neck lock and pulled him backwards. Meanwhile, the first policeman had managed to lift Collins to his feet.

Lindo coughed loudly, raspingly gasping for air as at last he began to breathe again. He pointed shakily to Detective Collins. "Him mussi mad. First him tell me seh he is the Swinger an' nex' t'ing me know, him tell me seh him is a donkey!"

Winston quickly let go of the detective and moved a couple of paces back. Collins simply sat on the floor staring straight ahead.

"The Swinger? Wha' happen then?" asked the older officer.

"Him seh nobody coulda ketch him 'cause him have the ability fe change up himself an' look like johncrow, donkey…anyt'ing, man. An' him seh if me didn't admit to the murders dem, dat he would kill me an' mek it look like an accident." Lindo rubbed at his neck. Keeping his eyes firmly on the detective he said, "Aarks him yuhself."

The duty officer turned to Detective Collins. "Is dis true, yuh is the Swinger?"

Collins didn't respond straight away but slowly, surely, he moved his head up and then down.

Winston gasped.

"Me tell yuh… yuh see, ah nuh lie me ah talk," said Lindo.

The police officers stared in disbelief. Detective Barnabas Collins, a murderer? It couldn't be true. But was it any less believable than the fact that Collins was crawling on all fours allowing the obeah man to ride him? They had witnessed that with their own eyes. The man must surely have gone mad. Everyone knew that you didn't fool around with obeah men! One way or another, Collins was a danger to public safety and had to be kept in custody.

As Winston and his partner led Detective Collins away to a separate cell, Lindo picked up the table and one of the chairs. He sat down and pulled out his pipe, placing it carefully on the table while he rummaged in his pockets for something to smoke. He packed the dried weed into the pipe's bowl and pressed it in hard. Then he lit up, put the pipe's stem to his mouth and inhaled deeply. How foolish these people were, trying to solve murders that couldn't be solved when all they needed to do was believe in the power of obeah.

He sat back in his chair and smiled conspiratorially. "You have yuh confession now, Detective Collins," said Lindo and, in a whisper, "if you do badness to the obeah man, dat badness gwine come back to you."

NEW!
Black Classics

From The X Press – an exciting collection of the world's great forgotten black classic novels. Many brilliant works of writing lie in dusty corners of libraries across the globe. Now thanks to Britain's leading publisher of black fiction, you can discover some of these fantastic novels. Over the coming months we will be publishing many more of these masterpieces which every lover of classic fiction will want to collect.

THE BLACKER THE BERRY by Wallace Thurman

Emma Lou was born black. Too black for her own comfort and that of her social-climbing wannabe family. Resented by those around her, she drifts from one loveless relationship to another in the search for herself and a place in a society where prejudice towards her comes not only from whites, but from her own race!

TRADITION by Charles W Chesnutt

In the years after the American Civil War, a small town in the Deep South struggles to come to terms with the new order. Ex-slaves are now respected doctors, lawyers and powerbrokers--And the white residents don't like it one bit! When a black man is wrongly accused of murdering a white woman, the black population, proud and determined, strike back.

IOLA by Frances E.W. Harper

The beautiful Iola Leroy is duped into slavery after the death of her father but manages to snatch her freedom back and start the long search for the mother whom she was separated from on the slave trader's block. She rejects the advances of a white man, who offers to relieve her from the "burden of blackness" by marrying her and eventually finds love and pride in her race.

THE CONJURE MAN DIES by Rudolph Fisher

Originally published in 1932, *The Conjure Man Dies* is the first known thriller by an African-American. Rudolph Fisher, one of the principal writers of the Harlem Renaissance, weaves an intricate story of a native African king, who settles in Harlem and becomes a fortune teller or 'Conjure Man'. When the old man is found dead the rumours start spreading. Things are made even more confusing when he turns up later, very much alive!

THE AUTOBIOGRAPHY OF AN EX-COLORED MAN
by James Weldon Johnson

Until his school teacher points out to him in no uncertain terms that he's a "nigger", the 'ex-colored man' believed that his fair skin granted him the privileges of his white class mates. The realisation of what life holds for him is at first devastating, but as he grows into adulthood, he discovers a pride in his blackness and the noble race from which he is descended. However a disturbing family secret is soon to shake up his world.

THE HOUSE BEHIND THE CEDARS
by Charles W. Chesnutt

Two siblings, Rena and John Walden, 'pass' for white in the Deep South as their only means of obtaining a share of the American dream. The deception poses a dilemma when Rena falls in love with a rich white man. Can love transcend racial barriers, or will the dashing George Tryon reject her the moment he discovers her black roots?

THE WALLS OF JERICHO by Rudolph Fisher

When black lawyer Fred Merrit buys a house in an exclusive white neighbourhood, he has to hire the toughest removal firm in Harlem to help him move in. That's when the comedy begins. A hilarious satire.

A LOVE SUPREME by Pauline Hopkins

Sappho Clark is beautiful and chaste, but guilt-ridden because of some dark secret in her past. Only a man with the greatest love for her will be prepared to overlook it. Will she find that man?

THE PRESIDENT'S DAUGHTER by William Wells Brown

Based on the much-repeated claim that Thomas Jefferson, founding father, slave owner and early president of the United States had fathered many slaves. Clotel, the president's beautiful daughter by his housekeeper is sold at slave market at the age of sixteen, in the shadows of the White House where her indifferent father presides.

Also Available *Black Classics*

Three more forgotten greats of black writing will be available from June 1996. Check out: *ONE BLOOD* by Pauline Hopkins, *JOY & PAIN* by Rudolph Fisher and *THE SOUL OF A WOMAN* by Harriet E. Wilson. Ask for details in any good bookshop. Only from *The X Press*.

Books with ATTITUDE

THE RAGGA & THE ROYAL by Monica Grant
Streetwise Leroy Massop and The Princess of Wales get it
together in this light-hearted romp.   £5.99

JAMAICA INC. by Tony Sewell
Jamaican Prime Minister, David Cooper, is shot down as he
addresses the crowd at a reggae 'peace' concert. But who pulled
the trigger and why?   £5.99

LICK SHOT by Peter Kalu
When neo-nazis plan to attack Manchester's black community
they didn't reckon on one thing...A black cop who doesn't give a
fuck about the rules!   £5.99

SINGLE BLACK FEMALE by Yvette Richards
Three career women end up sharing a house together and
discover they all share the same problem-MEN!   £5.99

MOSS SIDE MASSIVE by Karline Smith
When the brother of a local gangster is shot dead on a busy
Manchester street, the city is turned into a war zone as the drugs
gangs battle it out.   £5.99

BABY FATHER by Patrick Augustus
Four men come to terms with parenthood but it's a rough journey
they travel before discovering the joys in this smash hit.   £5.99

BABY FATHER 2 by Patrick Augustus
The sequel to the bestselling *Baby Father*. Johnny, Beres,
Linvall and Gussie are still trying to do the right thing with
regards to their kids and their relationships.

WHEN A MAN LOVES A WOMAN by Patrick Augustus
Campbell Clarke thought he would never fall in love again until he met
Dionne Owen. The only problem is that he's poor while she's from a
respected buppie family and she's about to get married to a rich guy! £5.99

Books with ATTITUDE

FETISH by Victor Headley
The acclaimed author of 'Yardie', 'Excess', and 'Yush!' serves another gripping thriller where appearances can be very deceiving! £5.99

PROFESSOR X by Peter Kalu
When a black American radical visits the UK to expose a major corruption scandal, only a black cop can save him from the assasin's bullet. £5.99

UPTOWN HEADS by R.K. Byers
Hanging with the homeboys in uptown New York where all that the brothers want is a little respect! A superb, vibrant humourous modern novel about the black American male. £5.99

OPP by Naomi King
How deep does friendship go when you fancy your best friend's man? Find out in this hot bestseller! £5.99

COP KILLER by Donald Gorgon
When his mother is shot dead by the police, taxi driver Lloyd Baker becomes a one man cop-killing machine. Hugely controversial but compulsive reading. £4.99

DANCEHALL by Anton Marks
Dancehall deejay Simba Ranking, is close to making it big-time in the world of ragga music until he meets an society woman with an uptown 'slam'. £5.99

GAMES MEN PLAY by Michael Maynard
Winston, Andre, Calvin and Marcus are friends who share the same passions and problems in life - sport and women! A novel about black men behaving outrageously but with frank honesty. They'll make you laugh, cry and get £5.99

WICKED IN BED by Sheri Campbell
Michael Hughes believes in 'loving and leaving 'em' when it comes to women. But if you play with fire you're gonna get burnt! £5.99